The
BEAGLE

EDITED BY
ANN PHILLIPS

BEST of
BREED

ACKNOWLEDGEMENTS

The publishers would like to thank the following for help with photography: Ann Phillips (Lanesend); Penny Carmichael (Kernebridge); Patience Walden (Nedlaw); Veronica Bradley and Ken Burgess (Dufosee); Sally Parker (Chapscroft); Mandy Bobbitt; Sue Leader; David Webster (Webline); Greg Knight (Rural Shots); AQIS Australian Government; Debbie Taylor; Susan Arden; Hearing Dogs for Deaf People, Pets As Therapy.

Cover photo: © Tracy Morgan Animal Photography (www.animalphotographer.co.uk)
Dog featured is Ch. Chapscroft Briar JW

Pages 14, 56 and 84 © Sabine Stuewer – Tierfoto (www.stuewer-tierfoto.de)
Page 22 © Australian Quarantine and Inspection Service

The British Breed Standard reproduced in Chapter 7 is the copyright of the Kennel Club and published with the club's kind permission. Extracts from the American Breed Standard are reproduced by kind permission of the American Kennel Club.

THE QUESTION OF GENDER
The 'he' pronoun is used throughout this book instead of the rather impersonal 'it', but no gender bias is intended.

First published in 2011 by The Pet Book Publishing Company Limited
The Granary, Bishton Farm, Tidenham, Chepstow, Gloucestershire NP16 7LJ

ISBN
978-1-906305-50-5
1-906305-50-1

Printed and bound in China through Printworks Int. Ltd.

CONTENTS

GETTING TO KNOW BEAGLES

Chapter 1

The Beagle is a medium-sized, short-coated hound, originally bred as a pack hound to hunt the hare while the field followed on foot. In modern times he has found his niche as a devoted family pet, but his pack origins should always be borne in mind, as the hunting instinct is never far beneath the surface.

PHYSICAL CHARACTERISTICS

The Beagle is a compact and sturdy animal. There should be no exaggerations in his physical make-up; standing four-square, this little hound displays moderation in all aspects of his being.

The Beagle is defined by his head, the large, low-set ears framing the skull, the dark brown or hazel eyes giving a mild, appealing expression. It is the expression that melts hearts when people first encounter the breed and moves people to smile if they pass a Beagle on the street.

SIZE AND WEIGHT

The desirable height for the breed, for both dogs and bitches in the UK and most of the rest of the world, is between 13-16 inches (33-40 cm) at the withers (top of the shoulder). The height in Beagles in America is divided into two groups: those under 13 inches and those between 13-15 inches (33-38 cm); anything outside these parameters will be eliminated in the show ring in that country.

Because of the considerable height difference within the breed, weight will vary according to the height and sex of a particular dog. The British Standard gives a very flexible, permissible height in Beagles, being three inches (7.5 cm) between the upper and lower desired limits. Consider those three inches in the context of a bitch of 13 inches (33 cm) and a dog hound of 16 inches (40 cm); the bitch will look very small compared with the dog. Thus, an average weight for a fully mature 15-inch (38-cm) dog hound would be 30-35 lbs (13.6-15.8 kg); bitches, being generally more petite, should weigh correspondingly less. Weight can be a problem and it is far healthier to have a slightly underweight Beagle than one tending to obesity. This is a breed that loves its food, so Beagle owners have to guard against those pleading eyes! The skeleton should be well covered, but you should be able to feel the ribs.

Many Beagles mature in body by the time they are 12 months old; others go through a gangly stage that lasts up to 18 months of age before they attain their adult weight.

BEAGLE COLOURS

Tricolour: Black, tan and white.

Lemon and white.

COLOURS

Beagles come in a variety of 'hound' colours. The most common, and the one usually associated with the breed by the general public, is tricolour (a combination of black, tan and white). Markings may appear in bold patches, sometimes with a black saddle merging into tan, with white on the muzzle, the legs and the tip of the tail. But there is no set pattern to a Beagle's markings.

Another colour that is seen more these days is the bicolour tan and white, the very pale version being termed lemon and white. What we in the UK call tan and white is often referred to as red and white in the USA and Australasia, but a true red and white hound does not occur very often.

Beagles also come in mottle and pied, be they tricolour or bicolour, and have the same range of colour combinations.

LIFE EXPECTANCY

Many Beagles live to a venerable age – I have had hounds that lived to be 15 and 16 years without ailing until their last days. Beagles are, in the main, healthy and active dogs; however, I have known Beagles who have died as young as five years, usually due to some form of cancer.

MOVEMENT

Beagles move with an effortless, trotting gait, covering the ground and, being bred to hunt, they can go all day. They have moments of wild activity – particularly when young – but, generally, they will spend their days pottering around the garden, visiting and revisiting sites of particular 'smelly' interest.

TYPICAL BEHAVIOUR

Beagles are naughty, on occasion wicked, charming, impossible bordering on stubborn, beguiling with their pleading brown eyes, at times infuriating, but totally lovable rogues with hearts of gold and minds of steel. Inquisitive creatures, they will investigate anything and everything that they encounter in their daily lives. Owners need to be one jump ahead, particularly with puppies, to check there are no lurking dangers to life and limb. A favourite 'play thing' for a small puppy is the lamp flex snaking across the floor – if chewed through while still plugged in, this can prove fatal.

Beagles love to dig and can excavate incredible craters in search of grubs, voles or other imaginary goodies – remember: food is the driving force combined with an incredible sense of smell! Beagles are fond of raw vegetables and, if unchecked, will dig their own from the vegetable garden. Fencing off precious flower-beds is a must if the gardener in the house is to retain his/her sanity. The green, plastic-coated 'border' wire is ideal for this, as it is unobtrusive to the eye, pushes into the ground and needs minimal support. I have used the 30-inch (76-cm) height variety for many years. Make sure it is in situ before your Beagle has access to the garden, as it is always more difficult to break an acquired habit.

A Beagle, particularly a bitch, will bury toys, bones and sometimes even biscuits to be retrieved as a delicacy at a later

The Beagle is ever alert for the next interesting sight, sound or smell.

date. Beagles do not generally retrieve to you, as they were bred to hunt and the quarry was not of interest to the hunt followers. Unlike the gundog breeds, who willingly retrieve to hand, if a Beagle steals, you will have to entice the object back with the offer of a greater prize than the one already in his possession.

Beagles are quick to learn and one of their many endearing habits is to work out that they will be rewarded for bringing something to you rather than dashing off with the trophy. This behaviour can manifest itself in the hound retrieving to order such things as windfall apples, and golf balls – if you live beside a golf course – all for the expected treat. Some years ago, I had a Beagle who would collect golf balls and store them under bushes. When he decided he wanted a treat, he would appear with one and keep on fetching them until he felt he had had enough food for the time being – stupid they are not!

There are occasions when a Beagle, on seeing something unusual for the first time – a hot-air balloon or even a flapping plastic bag, for example – can become quite timid and may bark furiously at whatever has startled him. It is then up to you, the pack leader, to reassure and calm the situation, so it is wise to keep some form of treat handy for such an eventuality. Remember, the Beagle was bred for hundreds of years to live amicably in a pack; therefore, the individual Beagle –

A Beagle looks to his owner for leadership.

as so many are these days – needs support in times of stress, as he does not have the rest of the pack around him. A Beagle that is taken out and about from a young age and introduced to a variety of sights and sounds should have no such problems with the everyday world.

THE BEAGLE MIND

Beagles are happy, social animals due, in no small part, to their pack ancestry, where they lived together in large numbers. Today the modern Beagle's pack is his human family and the young Beagle, on entering his new world, will look to you, his owners, for leadership. This leadership needs to start on day one or he will take on that role with great alacrity. The Beagle is an active dog, displaying stamina and determination in spades, and needs all this energy channelled into becoming the ideal family companion.

A Beagle dislikes being left alone for long periods and will leave you in no doubt of this by becoming destructive, noisy and very possibly dirty in the house. Do not let his diminutive size lull you into a false sense of security; a bored Beagle can wreak mega destruction in your house in a relatively short time. His intelligence needs challenging and channelling, particularly over the first six to 12 months of his life. You need to establish a bond with you, as leader, and your Beagle as faithful follower.

If you have children, they must be taught to respect the puppy's

Every Beagle is an individual – but most will respond to a bit of bribery.

space, in particular his bed, his toys and his food. Beagles are very tolerant and get on well with children and other family pets – they like the interaction, the games and the stimulation of being part of everything. Beagles do not thrive on solitude and boredom; in these situations they take the law into their own paws and can, if left unchecked, become unruly members of society.

Every Beagle has his own distinct personality. I have one who works things out, very much on his own terms; one who is biddable, prepared to follow and

will hold up his paws and admit 'he did it' even when it is patently clear he did not; and then there's the youngest member who is into everything, has no fear and thinks life is just a breeze.

BEAGLES AND CHILDREN

Beagles are very good with children. However, when a puppy is introduced to your family it is vital that young children do not think of him as a toy; they will need to be supervised when playing with him. A puppy's first teeth are like needles and a child's face or fingers could be

INTELLIGENCE, STAMINA AND GREAT DETERMINATION

Some Beagles are too intelligent for their own good! One such, named Stoker, resides with me. At a little over 12 weeks he discovered how to climb from the puppy pen and follow me, at great speed, ears flying like Snoopy, into the three-acre field to join in the fun. This resulted in him being carried round the field each morning until old enough to run with the big boys. This, of course, was the forerunner of working things out.

Stoker learnt very quickly that tapping the house door with his paws would gain him entry but, as he could not be seen at the door from inside the house, he started tapping the door and then moving to stand in front of the kitchen window, gazing intently for attention. The moment he spotted the 'doorkeeper' he would move back to the door, ready to enter.

One day he jumped at the kitchen door, caught the handle by accident – it levers downwards – and landed inside! He puzzled this through, perfected coming in, then turned his attention to going out. This he mastered within a couple of weeks by pulling down on the handle with his front feet, moving backwards on his hind legs and, bingo, the door opened – he has yet to learn how to close it after him!

He has a favourite soft toy – now minus two legs and a tail – that is taken outside at least once a day for 'exercise'. Once the game is over, he returns the toy to his bed – an indoor kennel – and closes the door (mine sleep in indoor kennels in the kitchen)! His list of achievements is endless and ongoing and, yes, he is a delight to live with – albeit, on occasion, challenging!

It did not take Stoker long to work out how to open the kitchen door.

A Beagle will get on well with children as long as mutual respect is established.

caught without the puppy realising what he has done.

Teach your children that when the puppy is in his bed he should be left alone. He needs rest and will wake refreshed and ready for more fun. The puppy should also be left alone at mealtimes. Children need to learn the correct way to handle a puppy, not pulling on his legs or his tail, poking at him with their fingers, or teasing him in any way. They must not be allowed to pick up the puppy; a wriggling pup is difficult to hold and he may be hurt if he is dropped.

After all the 'do nots', the good news is that your children and puppy will soon become firm friends. They will enjoy sitting together and having a cuddle, enjoying a game in the garden chasing a ball, and, later on, going for walks. If your children respect your puppy then your puppy will respect your children and they will become inseparable as they grow.

Resist the temptation of getting two puppies from the same litter – they will be more than twice the workload.

MORE THAN ONE?

This can be a vexing question, particularly when you first see a litter of bouncing Beagles and look into those deep, appealing eyes. It seems impossible to choose just one, but I would urge you to resist the temptation of taking on two. All the old arguments of being pack animals and needing a friend do not hold up against the practicalities of two littermates taking over your house.

Take one adorable baby home and teach him the ways of his new world, which will take all your time and patience. If there is a puddle (or worse!), you will know who did it; if something is chewed, you will know who did it; if there is a hole in the garden, you will know who did it... Then the appropriate action can be

taken in a firm but kindly manner. If you take home two babies, you will never know who did what – each will look at you pleadingly, denying all knowledge – and you will have a couple of hooligans on your hands.

Once your Beagle is the model of good behaviour, you can consider getting another, if your circumstances allow. You will find the new arrival has someone to look up to and, hopefully, you will be beginning to understand the Beagle mind.

Being a pack hound, a Beagle will thrive on company, so, if you decide to take on two of these fun-loving hounds – once the first is suitably manageable – you will need to consider the combination that is most likely to be compatible. In reality, it is a matter of personal preference

whether you choose a same-sex pair or opt for a male and a female, as, unlike some breeds, same-sex Beagles get on perfectly well. Personally, I favour male hounds as I find them more biddable. Bitches tend to be a bit more self-willed whereas the dogs seem to want to please. Having said that, no two Beagles are alike, although the basic breed characteristics will manifest themselves; this is mostly allied to their incredible sense of smell, their determination, stamina and great love of food.

If your preference is to have a dog and a bitch, then you will have to consider the consequences of the bitch coming into season twice a year and how you will cope with keeping them apart for at least three weeks, both financially and emotionally.

A Beagle will enjoy the company of other breeds – although he may 'borrow' some of their characteristics.
Photo © istockphoto.com/Andrea Krause.

You may not have the facilities to keep them separated at home, in which case you will need to kennel one or the other. You may also find they experience separation anxiety, as Beagles get very attached to their playmates.

The alternative is to have the bitch spayed – I would not advocate having a dog castrated in these circumstances, as if the bitch is entire, he will still howl and attempt to mount her; you will also be plagued by all the other male dogs in the vicinity. Spaying, in my opinion, should not be performed until the bitch is fully mature following her second season. This is a major operation, requiring a full anaesthetic, and should not be undertaken lightly. However, unlike people, dogs recover very quickly, possibly due to not having any pre-conceived ideas of how they should be feeling!

MIXING BREEDS

If you already own a dog of another breed and decide to add a Beagle to your household, it is likely that your new addition will take on some of the characteristics and the mind-set of the other breed, as this dog will become his role model.

I had a Beagle who lived much of his life with me in the company of Golden Retrievers; he retrieved, he swam, he walked at heel with no lead, and would be keen to greet any Golden he met – he thought that was what he was. Another Beagle spent his first six months with a Belgian Shepherd Dog (Groenendael) and copied many of this breed's traits.

LIVING WITH OTHER ANIMALS

Bearing in mind the 'pack' instinct, Beagles are generally amenable to living with cats and other different species. The new puppy should be introduced quietly to any other resident animals and not left unattended, particularly with cats, as they have very sharp claws and could do considerable damage to a pup. Equally, a puppy left alone with a pet mouse could have a similar traumatic effect on the mouse. Commonsense is the key. A word of warning: although he may be chums with the resident cat, he probably won't be with the cat next door!

AN IDEAL HOME

The ideal home for a Beagle is one where he can run and play in safety, where he is never left to his own devices, and where he cannot escape. This is, of course, the ideal home for any animal; however, we all know that the world is far from ideal and we can only strive to do the best with what we have.

Beagles need a well-fenced, secure garden or they will venture into pastures new to explore (remember his nose). This can be dangerous for the dog, particularly in a built-up area, and a menace to car drivers and local residents. The fencing should be high enough to deter the most agile of Beagles, with at least 6 inches (15 cms) dug into the ground to prevent tunnelling out. A Beagle should not be left alone for the whole day while the family is at work but should be brought up to accept short absences, particularly in the formative early weeks and months of his life. A Beagle will adapt to the family surroundings, be it town or country living, provided he gets regular exercise.

The Beagle's short coat does not require a lot of attention but will need a brush each day to remove the dead and shedding coat, otherwise clothes, carpets and furniture will show tiny, white hairs and non-doggy friends in dark clothes will be less than happy to visit in future. It is the nature of a Beagle's jacket that you only see the white hairs and these seem to come out in great profusion however little white hair your Beagle would appear to have! A Beagle should not expect food from the table at family mealtimes, but should be taught to go to bed – I advocate an indoor crate where he can be shut in when the need arises and where he knows he is safe and secure.

WORKING BEAGLES

When you collect your puppy, do not let the breeder try to pull the wool over your eyes by saying that the hunting instinct has been bred out of the Beagle – it most definitely has not! Beagles that live primarily in kennels are not often given the opportunity to follow a scent, giving a false impression of their capabilities. However, when given that opportunity, the majority will jump at the chance to follow the 'drag' and the real thing when out walking.

Both pet and show Beagles can revisit their pack ancestry and try out their 'scent' skills by joining in with organised working activities.

HUNTING HOUNDS
(By Alistair Parker, former Field Master of The Beagle Club Working Section)
Although our show and pet Beagles have for many generations been bred to the Breed Standard, as drawn up by the national kennel clubs, they all descend from hounds bred to hunt hare. Understandably, there are noticeable differences between those hounds bred purely to perform their original working purpose and those bred for the show ring. Nevertheless, breed enthusiasts have long known that a pet or show Beagle retains some

This is an easy breed to care for, as long as you give your Beagle the time and attention he deserves.

of the tenacious qualities of pack hounds and in 1963 a number of members of The Beagle Club in the UK joined up with the North Warwickshire pack, owned by Reg Wright, to satisfy their curiosity and see whether their hounds would work.

Encouraged by the results they looked into the feasibility of operating a working section on a more regular basis to simulate the hunting experience. Rather than hunt live quarry they decided to use an artificial line or drag. The hounds were clearly content to work such a line and proved to be so successful that in late 1963 the Kennel Club gave approval for The Beagle Club to award a

Working Certificate to those hounds judged to 'Enter to drag, give tongue and run free from riot.'

Nearly 50 years later The Beagle Club working section continues to thrive and holds regular meetings throughout the autumn and winter months to allow members to try to work their hounds. Some hounds are very enthusiastic, others less so, but all enjoy their day out in the country.

The scent is a mixture of aniseed and vegetable oil, diluted in a ratio of about 1:20, sprinkled on a piece of old, wet towelling. This is attached to a length of twine, which the line layer

literally drags behind him as he runs (or perhaps walks briskly) around a field. Lines may typically be between one and two miles in length. In order better to simulate the movement of a hare, the line layer will change direction or lift the line for a time. Hounds are usually released in two groups: the proven workers first followed shortly by the more novice hounds. It is not a race, as the first back may not have followed a true line. If a testing line has been laid, it is easy to see those that are working properly, as they will follow the changes in direction or, where the line has been lifted, stop and cast around

The Beagle retains a strong instinct to work in a pack and follow a line. These hounds are from the Royal Agricultural College, Cirencester, which is a registered pack in the UK.

to find the scent and then continue.

The highlight of the year remains the field trials that hounds qualify to attend by virtue of having attended and fully participated at meetings during the year. The trials are judged by two Masters of Hounds who have years of experience in watching hounds at work. They award marks for the attributes described in the words on the Working Certificate plus up to two discretionary marks for those hounds who show particularly strong working attributes and pack leadership.

The prize awarded is a much-coveted Working Certificate for which competition is always stiff – out of maybe 36 qualifiers only six or eight hounds will be awarded one in any year.

It may seem a little removed from the professionally run packs of today, but we should

AUSTRALIAN DRAG HUNTING

In Australia, Beagle enthusiasts are keen to see their hounds fulfilling their original function, and the sport of drag hunting is proving very popular in New South Wales, Victoria and South Australia. In Queensland they 'lure' hunt, using a decoy, instead of live game, in an enclosed area. The hounds are released one at a time to test their response to the movement of the lure. There is no hunting in the Northern Territory, as it is too hot!

Brian and Lesley Childs, of the Brialey Beagles, give a first-hand account of drag hunting in New South Wales:

"We first started the scent weekend seven years ago as a recognised activity of the Beagle Club of New South Wales.
The 'hunt' is held the second weekend in July each year, at Bimbadeen, a huge property on the outskirts of Cootamundra township. It has become known as the Christmas in July Scent Drag.

"The event is for Beagles only – most of the hounds are family pets more accustomed to sleeping on their owners' loungers! We also have a few show dogs, who prove that they are not only good-looking but talented, too! Following the scent comes naturally to the hounds, though we have had a few who refuse to follow. They stand and happily watch the others go off into the distance, then turn around and walk back to their owners!

"We have had up to 45 Beagles at the event. Saturday consists of six drags of varying lengths from 1-3 kilometres (0.6-1.8 miles) and on Sunday we do another six. Each drag is over clean ground – thankfully Bimbadeen is a huge property!

"The 'drag' is prepared days ahead. A bullock's liver is cooked very slowly over low heat, with garlic. The day before the drag, the liver is placed in a hessian bag, which is then soaked overnight in the liquid used to cook the liver. The morning of the event, the drag is transported (very carefully!) to Bimbadeen. Past experience has taught us that the liquid is rather potent, and it is extremely difficult to remove the smell from the car!

"The hounds are all kept on their leashes as the final part is played out. The bag containing the drag is attached to a rope, which is in turn attached to a quad bike. The rider of the bike then heads off into the bush with the drag bouncing behind. By this stage the noise from the hounds is deafening – the old timers know exactly what is remember that Beagling had its own origins in the enthusiast bringing their hounds to meetings and making up so called 'trencher-fed packs'. The term "trencher fed," is often used in 19th century literature to refer to the old hound management system in which hounds were kept by individuals, often farmers at their home, and then brought to a meet to form a pack with other hounds on a hunting day. The trencher was a slab of bread that lined a wooden plate and was fed to the hounds after the meal.

Almost every Beagle in the show ring or in pet ownership today can trace his ancestry back to trencher-fed hounds with names like 'Mr Johnson's Marvel 1892' or 'the Hon C Fitzwilliam's Frugal'. Today's working section hounds fare rather better than their ancestors but still carry on the long tradition of the trencher-fed pack.

Beagles are enthusiastic participators in the sport of drag hunting.

going to happen, and their excitement is contagious! The hounds are kept on lead, until the bike rider, who is hidden from view by the scrub, returns to a predetermined point. This is no mean feat with highly excited, exuberant dogs bounding up and down on the spot. Inevitably, we have a few slip-ups, where over-excited dogs either slip their collars or simply pull away from their owners. Laying the track in this way ensures the hounds are scenting and not merely chasing the drag.

"On the given signal, the hounds are released. They are a joy to behold, noses down, giving voice as they stream out along the valley floor. We catch glimpses of them as they burst into a clearing – it is a very stirring sight.

"After a few runs, the pack breaks up into a set pattern: the leaders, who do all the work casting for the correct trail, the main body of the hunt and, lastly, the stragglers at the rear. Some hounds are definite leaders and the others instinctively follow them. I might add that the most consistent pack leader is a Champion show dog, who has done well at Specialty level and has won the odd best gaited class!

"Saturday afternoon, after the day's drags have been completed, we all meet at a park in town and walk through and around Cootamundra. We have had up to 55 Beagles on this walk through the township, and we walk at least four kilometres. It is quite a sight to see that many Beagles of all shapes and colours walking up the main street of a small country town. We invariably stop traffic, and each year we have many wonderful comments from the public.

"By the end of the day, we have some very tired, but very content hounds, who are happy to curl up in their beds and snore the night away! Their humans then retire to a wonderful Christmas dinner and great company. Sunday sees more drags. By mid-afternoon, hounds and humans are ready to head home, with plans already being made to meet again next year!"

AMERICAN SMALL PACK OPTION BEAGLE HUNTING

Josh Sink and Ron Anderson, who regularly hunt, give details of the American scene.

All American Kennel Club (AKC) registered Beagles can enter field trials for Championship wins and points culminating in a Field Trial title for the successful hound. The trials are held under the auspices of AKC member clubs that are licenced by the AKC to hold such trials. The Beagles entered hunt either wild rabbit or hare. There are five permissible formats that a club can choose when organising a trial: Brace, Small Pack, Brace to Small Pack and Small Pack Option (SPO). All formats run under the same standards with different rules.

Taking the AKC licensed SPO Field Trial, as an example, the hounds are first divided by sex and size. There are classes for 13 inch and 15 inch dog hounds and for 13 inch and 15 inch bitches. Of these classes, the 13 inch hounds might be considered the expert class, due to their ability to turn more quickly than their larger cousins, but top hounds can be found in all four classes.

In a typical scenario, they may be seventy 13-inch dog hounds at a trial. They are divided into packs of no more than seven hounds, and this is done on a random basis. There are always

In the US, Beagles are judged in small packs to assess their ability to follow a scent.

two judges for a trial.

The first pack, their handlers and the judges, head out for a simulated rabbit hunt. Game is found and the pack gives pursuit. Now the judges have to determine which dogs are doing the best on that day. Normally the swinging or skirting hounds are ordered up first and, next, the dogs that are at the back not getting any rabbits are eliminated. This usually leaves a few dogs in the middle who are really running the rabbit. Once the judges are satisfied and agree on the scores, the Beagles head back for a rest, and the next pack is cast.

After the judges have looked at all the packs, they will announce which dogs will need to come back for a second series. This would typically be between 24 and 35 hounds, who are, again, divided into packs of no more than seven, and the same process as the first series is followed. After

the second series there is usually a third series followed by the final pack, called the winners pack. At the end of this final pack, the judges will name four hounds who will each receive points towards their Field Trial title. They will then designate a Next Best Qualifier; this hound will receive a ribbon but no points. Points towards the title of Field Trial Champion are awarded where there are six or more starters in a class:

- The winner receives one point for each starter
- The dog in second gets half a point for each starter
- The dog in third gets a third of a point per starter
- The dog in fourth gets a quarter of a point per starter.

A starter is an entered hound that has not been disqualified for whatever reason, including failing to go under the height measure for his class. A hound needs three wins and 120 points to gain his title. This could be achieved at back-to-back trials or it could take several years – there is no time limit, he just needs the wins! A Field Trial Champion that holds his Show Champion title is termed a Dual Champion, if he also has an Obedience title he becomes a Triple Champion.

Working Beagles now look significantly different from those bred from show lines. *Photo: Greg Knight.*

THE GREAT DIVIDE

All modern-day Beagles owe their origins to the pack hounds, but the show/pet Beagle of today differs greatly in his physical make-up from the contemporary pack Beagle. Pack Beagles are bred to hunt a specific 'country' – that is, they are bred for the type of terrain they will hunt over, be it downland or the high hills. A larger, rangier hound will be required for negotiating the type of ground encountered in the north of the UK – the stone walls and high stiles of the North Yorkshire moors, for example, whereas a smaller, faster hound will be better suited to the less challenging landscape further south.

Show/pet Beagles (I term these together, as most pet Beagles are from 'show' stock) are bred to the Breed Standard and do not have to take account of where they live to fulfil their function in life. Thus, the Beagle you see in the street will generally have more bone, be slightly heavier in build with longer, lower-set ears and a less snipey head than those seen when out hunting. The pack hound has, by definition, to be an athlete to fulfil his raison d'etre.

Many show breeders still bear in mind the hunting ancestry of their hounds and try to ensure their Beagles are fit and healthy and, if required, could hunt all day. You will not encounter a pack hound entered at a Kennel Club licensed show any more than you will see a show hound at a show run under the rules of the Association of Masters of Harriers and Beagles. However, a Beagle which has won a first prize at a show held by the above organisation is eligible for entry at Crufts. None such Beagle has been entered there in recent years.

VERSATILE BEAGLES

The Beagle is an intelligent dog, and, in the right hands, he can be trained to a high standard and perform a number of different tasks.

QUARANTINE (SNIFFER) BEAGLES

Australia, New Zealand and the USA employ Beagles to check passengers and their luggage at airports to detect the importation of illegal food substances, usually fruit and meat products. Beagles are thought to be the ideal breed for this, as they are non-threatening to people, friendly, and have the most amazing noses. They are trained to run over the suitcases as they are unloaded

The Beagle's amazing sense of smell is put to good use in airports, detecting food substances which have been imported illegally.

from the plane, and to sit beside any suspicious case, bag or person to alert their handlers to a possible illegal substance.

A friend of mine was stopped at Brisbane airport by a Beagle, who sat and gazed intently at her handbag. She knew she did not have any food but then remembered she had taken a banana on to the plane and had eaten it during the flight. To the Beagle, there was still a hint of scent in the bag!

Beagles used by the various customs services are generally selected from and donated by members of the public and not bred specifically for the job. Breed clubs in Australia have been particularly helpful to the Australian Quarantine and Inspection Service, though it is

fair to say that very few breeders donate a dog as, if the dog fails his very intensive training, he will be put in a pool of dogs for rehoming and will not be returned to the breeder, as he has become the property of the Government.

Successful recruits may be Beagles that have proved too much of a handful as a family pet who need their energies channelled into a more rewarding (for the dog) lifestyle. These hyperactive hounds can be very successful as 'sniffer' dogs and form a great bond with their handlers, but they live in kennels when not working, as it is thought that living in homes with the smell of cooking could upset their highly specialised scent training. When their working lives

are over they will, however, be found suitable homes.

THERAPY BEAGLES

Beagles are very successful as therapy dogs. Their medium size, short coats and mild, happy nature are ideal characteristics for working with elderly, sick or disabled people. They are welcomed in hospitals and care/nursing homes, and the patients/residents look forward to the weekly visits. Each dog is assessed as to his suitability for working in this area, temperament being of paramount importance. The owner must have the right attitude to work with people in this environment and be able to demonstrate close control of their dog at all times. The dog and owner work as a team with no outside assistance once they have passed the assessment.

SUMMING UP

Beagles are loyal, versatile little hounds with a big personality. They are intelligent and determined, which makes them a challenge but also a delight to own. I would be being economical with the truth if I said they fitted in with every lifestyle – they do not – they thrive on company and stimulation. They will live happily in an urban environment provided they get plenty of exercise and attention, but they are countrymen at heart and this should be borne in mind. However, once you have owned and cherished a Beagle, you will never want another breed in your life.

HELPING HOUND

Ralph is a therapy dog, owned by Chelsea Macklin in New Zealand. He attends a day care centre with Chelsea, and also visits clients in their own homes. The clients are both physically and mentally disabled – some from birth with conditions such as severe autism; others have suffered brain damage as a result of car accidents, or drug and alcohol abuse. A number of clients suffer from Alzheimer's disease. Ages range from early 20s to late 70s; Ralph mainly works with the older clients.

Chelsea explains Ralph's role and the benefits he can bring:

"Ralph is a 20-month-old Beagle, and, because he is a smaller breed, it is easier for some of the clients who are in wheelchairs to interact with him. He is also less intimidating if people are fearful of bigger dogs.

"There are a number of tasks that clients can get involved with:

- Brushing the dogs, which is really good for their movement.
- Bathing the dogs.
- Taking the dogs for walks around the garden or down the road to the park.
- Some clients take the dogs into town and go shopping. They are often stopped by passers-by who want to stroke the dogs, which provides a good opportunity for the clients to socialise and be part of the community.
- Some of the dogs, like Ralph, are a handy size and can be lifted on to the lap of a client in a wheelchair, giving the opportunity for lots of cuddles.

"Pet therapy sessions give the clients something to look forward to, and it gives them something to talk about with their carers, family and friends. When the clients are with the dogs, they are calm and relaxed.

"Not every dog is suited to working with clients with learning difficulties, who may, unintentionally, be slightly rough or insensitive when handling a dog. These dogs must have the right temperament, a laid-back attitude and an understanding of the environment and the situation they are put in.

"Ralph is a great therapy dog because he is small. He has a laidback attitude, loves being around all types of people and he loves being cuddled and given lots of attention. Ralph can also pick up vibes from the clients when they have had enough; he will walk away and go and be with someone else. This is not easy; many dogs are prone to be demanding and will paw at the clients for more attention.

"It is amazing to see the difference a dog can make to clients, modifying challenging behaviour, as well as providing love and affection, which is so badly needed."

Ralph: A very special Beagle who enhances the lives of many people.

THE FIRST BEAGLES

Chapter 2

Although the Beagle is generally regarded as a British breed, its origin, however obscure, is to be found outside the British Isles. The breed evolved from small hounds that were used for hunting small game in southern Europe, and in Greece in particular.

Evidence of this comes from the Greek author Xenophon, who was born about 433BC. After retiring from his military duties, he lived in Corinth where he wrote books and followed field sports. He kept a pack of hounds and is reputed to have given each a name and, like a good present-day Master of Hounds, he was able to recognise every one.

The method of hunting in those days commenced when the game – usually hares or rabbits – was driven from cover by beaters making a lot of noise and waving sticks. The beaters were followed by the hounds, who used scent and sight to drive the game towards nets, which were raised by concealed huntsmen. Just as is done today, the huntsmen hunted on foot rather than on horseback, which was the custom with larger game, such as deer. Illustrations found on pottery of this period show there were two types of hounds: small ones with thick muzzles and long ears, and a longer-legged hound with a slim and more pointed muzzle and shorter ears.

The Romans acquired the small hounds, which accompanied their legions throughout Europe and eventually to Britain, supplying the soldiers with hares and rabbits to eat. It is not certain if there were any small hunting hounds native to Britain when the Romans arrived, but Captain Otho Paget, described as the 'Dean of all Beagles' wrote:

"There were, however, in England packs of Beagles before the time of the Romans and it is on record that Pwyll, a Prince of Wales and contemporary of King Arthur, had a special breed of white hounds of great excellence."

It has also been claimed that the rough-coated Kerry Beagle in southern Ireland was in existence before the Romans arrived.

The hounds left by the Romans were later joined by larger hounds from Normandy, but for the next few centuries the more popular form of hunting was on horseback with deer, boar and wolves as the quarry. In the 14th century, Chaucer mentions in his *Canterbury Tales* "small houndes" belonging to the Prioress and, in Tudor times, Queen Elizabeth I

The stirring sight of a pack of Beagles in full cry.

Photo: Greg Knight.

had a pack of "singing Beagles", a name inspired when they gave tongue. These Beagles were supposed to have been small enough to fit inside a lady's gauntlet, and were referred to as 'Glove Beagles'. Another royal reference came from James I who referred to his wife as his "deare little Beagle", apparently as a term of affection!

HUNTING DOGS

British colonists are well known for taking their hobbies and interests to various parts of the British Empire in which they settled, so it was not surprising to find Beagle packs in South Africa, India, Ceylon, Australia and New Zealand.

In the 1860s, General Rowlett of Illinois imported some British pack hounds and started hunting them in the USA. Eventually these American packs were regulated by the National Beagle Club of America, formed in 1887, to organise field trials of packs engaged in hunting cottontail rabbits.

During the next few centuries

the role of the Beagle as a hunting dog in Britain changed very little. They were kept in packs all over the country; some colleges maintained packs, some were owned by private gentry but they were rarely kept as pets. Each Master of Hounds had his own ideas on the type and size required, usually dictated by the type of country to be hunted. To a lesser degree this is true today.

In the 18th and 19th centuries this difference of opinion led to many variations in type from the short, cobby little hounds, short in muzzle with heavy dewlaps, to the lighter-built hounds with longer legs and bodies. The *Sportsman's Diary,* published in 1800, defines the Beagle thus:

"Hunting dogs, of which there are several sorts, viz the Southern Beagle which is something less than the deep-mouthed hound, and something thicker and shorter. The Northern or Cat Beagle, which is smaller and finer than the Southern Beagle and is a hard runner. These two Beagles, by crossing, breed an excellent sort of Beagle not bigger than a lady's lap-

dog which makes pretty diversion when hunting the coney, and also the small hare when the weather be dry but by reason of the smallness this sort is not serviceable."

For more than 200 years Beagles had been bred to do a full day's work in the field. No Master of Hounds wanted a hound whose feet were flat or whose forelegs were not straight so that it tired easily; no Master wanted one with a narrow ribcage restricting the use of its lungs, no Master wanted a hound which could not get its nose to the ground to use its amazing scenting ability, and no Master wanted one with weak or crooked hindquarters which reduced its driving power. Because large numbers of hounds were kept together in kennels no Master wanted any which fought with each other or were difficult to feed, and, of course, no Master wanted a disobedient hound. Accordingly, Masters drafted hounds in and out of their kennels in order to achieve the qualities they were seeking. This standard was then maintained by careful line-breeding over the years. This 'fit for purpose' policy, which started so long ago, has produced a hound which today is noted for its health and sociability.

PROMOTING THE BREED

During the middle of the 19th century, the breed was in danger of losing its distinctive characteristics and becoming a miniature Foxhound. Controversially, a few Masters started to exhibit their hounds at hound shows where the variety of size and type became apparent, with each Master declaring his pack to be the most desirable.

To settle the arguments and bring in more uniformity the

James Phillips with one of his four sons, Glyn, photographed in 1897. The Beagle is typical of the smaller 'pocket Beagles', which was favoured by ladies of the time.

WHAT'S IN A NAME?

The small hounds were given no specific name by the Greeks, Romans, Normans or Saxons. In the 11th century the name 'Kennetty' was used for hounds of similar size; 'Rache' was used for the larger hounds. In the 15th century 'Hayreies' and 'Hayrers' were used for those harrying game, eventually becoming Harriers.

The first recorded use of the name 'Beagle' appears to be in about 1475 in The Squire of Low Degree in which it is written: "With theyr Beagles in that place and seven score Raches at his rechase."

The origin of the name is obscure, but various opinions have been expressed. Some believe it to be derived from the Old English 'Begle', others prefer the Old French 'Beigh' or the Celtic 'Beag', all of which mean 'small'. Another opinion is that Beagle is the Anglicised version of the French word 'Begeule', meaning 'gaping or deep throat', a reference to the Beagle's unique voice.

In the early 19th century the word 'Beagle' was used to mean a spy, presumably someone who sniffed out things, but a more pleasant memory is HMS Beagle, the ship used by the famous naturalist Charles Darwin on his voyages of discovery between 1831 and 1836.

breed's activities became organised by two separate bodies. In 1891 the Association of Master Harriers and Beagles took the responsibility of co-ordinating the activities of the hunting packs, and a year earlier The Beagle Club was formed under the auspices of the Kennel Club to promote the breed for sporting purposes and the exhibition of Beagles at shows. In 1892 it produced the first Standard of Points for the breed, which has remained virtually the same for more than a hundred years.

END OF AN ERA

As the 20th century progressed, hunting activities started to decline in Britain with many packs being disbanded or merged. Private packs almost entirely

disappeared because they became too expensive to maintain. At the end of the century, political pressure threatened the future of all hunting with dogs in Britain, causing the number of packs to be reduced to 62 in 2010.

The method of hunting used today is different from that used by the Ancient Greeks. Huntsmen still follow the hounds on foot, not on horseback, but nets are not used, the hounds being allowed to make the kill. Beagling has been described as 'the art of venery at its very highest'. There is a very strict code of conduct to be followed by everyone taking part. Huntsmen wear a uniform consisting of a jacket, in most packs green in colour, with different buttons or lapel badges to identify each pack, white

trousers, short black boots and a dark green or black cap. A whip is used to keep the hounds on the scent of their quarry, hence the use of the word 'whip' in parliamentary matters.

Despite political and financial restrictions, which have caused a few packs to disband, Britain is still the leading country for hunting live hares in the traditional manner. During recent years some illustrious names, such as Bolebrook, Warwickshire, Eton College, Halstead Place, Trinity College and the New Forest have become synonymous for good hunting and Champion hounds.

In the USA, well over 100 clubs are engaged in competitive field trial activities hunting cotton tail rabbits, whereas fewer than 30 hunt hare in the traditional manner. Two famous packs, the Treweryn (founded in 1924) and the Nantucket (founded in 1925) merged in 1964 to form the Treweyn-Nantucket pack. Other packs with a fine reputation for hunting include: Sir Sister, Bryn Mawr, Holly Hill, Windholme and Somerset and Wheatley. There is also a considerable number of small, private packs that are not regulated and their hounds are not registered.

In Scandinavia, where field trial success is essential for hounds to become Champions, there is plenty of hunting by individuals – but their quarry is usually fox, wolf or deer.

The Beagle Club of Transvaal in South Africa has a small working section, as does the New Zealand

By tradition, Beagle packs are followed on foot.

Beagle Club in the South Island. Sadly, the few private packs in India and Sri Lanka seem to have disappeared.

THE SHOW SCENE

The 20th century also saw a big increase in a new activity – the exhibition of Beagles at shows held under Kennel Club rules. Early pioneers were Mrs Stockley and Mrs Reynolds, whose hounds were very closely related to hunting stock. Gradually, more Beagles were seen in the show ring, but the First World War slowed things down and shows ceased until 1920.

In 1926 the first Beagle gained the title of Champion under the Kennel Club rules then in force. It was the bitch, Belton Scornful, and was followed by 11 more Champions until war again stopped shows being held between 1940 and 1945 when they were restarted largely due to the efforts of the Viscount Chelmsford.

When they were resumed the hounds were still closely descended from working pack hounds, the most successful being found in the Limbourne and Acregreen kennels. The then secretary of The Beagle Club, Douglas Appleton, used hunting stock to produce his early Appeline Champions Matchless, Glider, Rocket and Gaylass.

Notable Beagles bred by hunting packs appear in the pedigrees of those successful in the show ring following the Second World War. These include:

Warwickshire Triumph: A prolific winner in the 1940s.

Halstead Place Searcher (1905): A small tricolour dog described by Otho Paget as being "responsible for more good-looking stock than any Beagle that had ever lived."

Christ Church Signet (1928): A 15-inch dark badger-pied bitch that never won a Champion Cup

but was an excellent brood bitch and won the Brood Bitch class at Peterborough in 1931.

Bolebrook (Dummer) Woldsman (1941): A large lemon and white hound who won the Champion Cup in 1950. The sire of Eton College Woodman.

Eton College Woodman (1945): A big tricolour dog who won the Champion Cup in 1946.

Springfield Tranquil (1945): A small brood bitch whose value was curtailed by the war but her progeny proved very successful.

Warwickshire (Radley) Triumph (1947): A 15-inch hound of a peculiar silvery badger-pied colour. He won every class open to him, including the Champion Cup in 1949.

SOARING POPULARITY

In the 1950s an explosion took place in the registration of Beagles. In 1954 there were only 154 registered in the UK, but five years later the number had shot up to 1,092, and then 2,047 in 1962. A peak was reached in 1969 when 3,979 registrations made the Beagle one of the most popular of all breeds. During the same period membership of The Beagle Club increased some 25 times to nearly 500, most of whom were engaged in breeding for exhibition in the show ring.

INFLUENTAL BEAGLES

Pictured left to right: Ch. Barvae Varner, Ch. Barvae Paigan – widely regarded as the father of modern Beagles – and Ch. Barvae Ponder, all owned by Gladys Clayton.

Ch. Forradon Appeline Beeswing: Reserve Best in Show Crufts 1965. Owned by Leonard Pagliero and Pam Harris.

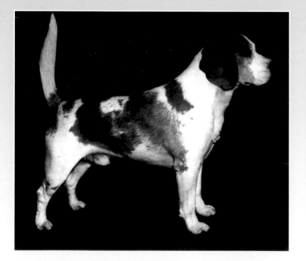

Ch. Houndsmark Manful: Winner of the Hound Group, Crufts 1970.

Photo: Diane Pearce.

Ch. Southcourt Wembury Merryboy: Winner of 14 Challenge Certificates, 10 with Best of Breed, 9 Reserve CCs, and the Hound Group, Darlington, 1970.

Photo: Cooke.

Ch. Dialynne Gamble (sire Am. Ch. Appeline Validay Happy Feller (imp. USA), dam Ch. Dialynne Nettle). Gamble had a significant influence on the breed in the 1970s & 80s, siring 26 UK champions and many more overseas.

Patricia Sutton with Ch. Rossut Foreman (born in 1971 by Rossut Gaffer – sire of 3 Champions – out of Ch Rossut Colinbar Phantom – dam of 2 Champions). Ch. Rossut Foreman was the top winning dog of his day with a total of 27 CCs, 17 Res CCs, four Hound Group wins and one Res Best in Show at a General Ch. Show. He was Res Best Veteran in the prestigious Pedigree Chum Veteran Stakes in 1979 and 1980.

TOP BREEDERS, TOP DOGS

Beagles being bred for the show ring were now several generations from hunting stock. Gladys Clayton (Barvae) imported Benroe Wrinkles, a prolific sire from Canada, and Thelma Gray (Rozavel) pursued her aim of breeding small Beagles by importing stock from the USA. Other leading breeders during this decade were: Joan Whitton (Tavernmews), Douglas and Carol Appleton (Appeline), Catherine Sutton (Rossut), Wyn Mahoney (Crestamere), Pamela Harris and Leonard Pagliero (Forrardon) and Diana Brown (Raimex).

Prominent Champions included: Twinrivers Garland (1961), Appeline Top Ace (1962), Wendover Billy (1961), Rossut Triumphant (1964), Raimex Tally (1967), Crestamere Orchid (1968), Rossut Gaiety (1968), Southcourt Wembury Merry Boy (1969) and Forrardon Foxtrot (1968).

During the next 10 years the picture changed little, but there were more opportunities to create new Champions because the Kennel Club increased the number of qualifying shows at which Challenge Certificates could be won. The Dialynne kennels of Marion Spavin was the most successful but was closely challenged by Crestamere and Rossut. The newer Dufosee kennels of Veronica and David Bradley started producing winning hounds. Dolly Macro with her Deaconfield Beagles was a well-known figure in the show ring.

Top-winning hounds during this period: Ch. Dialynne Gamble (1971), Ch. Dufosee Bonnie Girl (1972), Ch. Rossut Foreman (1973), Ch. Southcourt Hatchet (1974), Ch. Kernebridge Young Jolyon (1975), Ch. Dufosee Harris Tweed (1976), Ch. Pinewood Crib of Webline (1977), Ch. Beacott Buckthorn (1977), Ch. Jesson Fencer (1978) and Ch. Pancrest Scotch Mist (1979). In 1981 Ch. Beacott Buckthorn was Hound Group winner at Crufts.

Ch. Kernebridge Young Jolyon JW, born in 1972 (Sire Ch Lanesend Tallarook, Dam Rossut Chit Chat of Kernebridge). He was the winner of 5 CCs and Hound Group winner at the 1975 Birmingham National Championship Show. He took several Best in Show awards at breed club and general Open shows. *Photo: Diane Pearce.*

Pictured left to right: Ch. Rossut Sunset (Born 1974, by Ch. Rossut Foreman X Ch. Crestamere Twilight of Rossut in 1974) being shown by Pat Sutton, and Ch. Pinewood Crib of Webline (winner of four CCs and sire of several winners). The judge in the centre is Patricia Clayton.

AMERICAN INFLUENCE

The year 1958 proved very important for the development of the Beagle as the first American imports were released from quarantine. Mrs J. Beck and Mrs T. Gray imported Am. Ch Renoca's Best Showman, a small 12½-inch (31-cm) hound who was a big winner in the States, where he had become one of the youngest Champions. Am. Ch. Rozavel Ritter's Sweet Sue, a 12½-inch (31-cm) daughter of Am. Ch. Thornridge Wrinkles, and her daughter by Am. Ch. Johnson's Fancy King, the 12½-inch (31-cm) Ch. Rozavel Ritter's Miss Babe, joined the Rozavel kennels of Mrs. Gray. Mrs Beck brought over Am. Ch. Letton Wynnstay's Citation. The other

import was Mr. Douglas Appleton's Appeline Dancer of Camlyn. Mrs G. Clayton went to Canada for her import. Barvae Benroe Wrinkles was the son of the famous Ch. Thornridge Wrinkles, sire of more than 90 Champions in America and Canada. Thornridge Wrinkles was a very important and dominant sire who really stamped his stock. His son Barvae Benroe Wrinkles had a huge influence on the breed in Britain . The next dog that Mr Douglas Appleton imported was the big winner, Can. Am. and Eng. Ch Appeline Top Ace. He too proved a most dominant sire and produced stock of exceptional quality. Later in the Sixties Douglas Appleton was to bring over from the States Ch.

Appeline Validay Happy Feller who was to prove an important sire in the breed.

Marion Spavin's world famous Ch. Dialynne Gamble was the result of two lines of good breeding, being particularly line bred on his dam's side. Ch. Dialynne Nettle was the result of a half brother half sister mating, both being by Ch. Dialynne Huntsman, and he was by the import Barvae Benroe Wrinkles. Gamble himself was by the American import Ch. Appeline Validay Happy Feller, so producing a pedigree that was strongly American influenced.

Catherine Sutton began her kennel of Rossut Beagles by buying in several puppies from Mrs. English, who had a private

SCIENTIFIC RESEARCH

A dark period in the history of the Beagle coincided with its rise in popularity when scientists found it necessary to use live animals for research purposes. It was the very qualities of size and sociability that made the Beagle their breed of choice for experiments. Heated arguments about the need for these experiments took place and, sadly, a few prominent breeders covertly supplied laboratories with puppies. Eventually, public opinion led to tighter government control and reduced, but not eradicated, this undesirable activity in Britain. Much less occurs, but trafficking in Beagle puppies still continues in some Far Eastern countries.

This is the reason why a reputable breeder always interrogates a prospective puppy buyer in order to ensure the puppy is going to a good home, and not to a laboratory or puppy farm. Anyone asked lots of question should realise this and be grateful. The breeder is not being nosey but is taking sensible precautions. It is another reason why no one should buy an unseen puppy advertised on the internet.

pack in Norfolk. One of the most influential dogs was Ch. Rossut Triumphant who was out of Rossut Joker and Rossut Fashion (the latter being sired by Ch. Rozavel Mighty Dollar, who came over from America 'in utero' when Am. Ch Rozavel Ritter's Sweet Sue was imported in whelp). Triumphant lived up to his name, winning 23 CCs and becoming the first of four Beagles that went Best in Show at general Championship Shows for the Rossut kennel when he won Best in Show at Bournmouth in 1965. In his show career he also won the Hound Group at LKA, Birmingham City and SKC, as well as Best in Show at The Beagle Club Championship Show.

It is interesting that the majority of the top winning kennels of the Sixties used American imports and these outcrosses really improved the style and quality of the British Beagles. This is borne out when you look at the pedigrees of the Champions that were made up in those years. The vast majority were by an American import, or at the very least, had them in their pedigree in the second or third generation.

THE EIGHTIES AND NINETIES

In the last two decades of the 20th century, more and more Beagles were being exhibited and competition between breeders was keener than ever. In 1982 Catherine Sutton imported an American Champion, Graadtres Hot Pursuit, nicknamed 'Corkie', who produced several Champions for Andrew Brace's Tragband kennels, and in 1984 the last of the Appeline line gained his title – Ch. Pin Oaks Dynasty of Appeline had Dialynne blood in his pedigree. In Wales, Mal Phillips' Ch. Fertrac Brandy found success in the show ring and as a sire. The Jesson kennels of Honor Eades produced several Champions including Saddler, Lancer, Thrifty, Quaintly & Quester. The top-winning Beagle in 1995, 1996, 1997 and 1998 was Dialynne-bred but owned and exhibited by Andrew Brace. Ch. Dialynne Tolliver of Tragband, nicknamed 'Mikey', became the breed's record holder with 33 Challenge Certificates and the winner of four

Ch. Fertrac Brandy, born in 1985 (Sire Ch. Solomon of Dialynne, Dam Ch. Fertrac Anika). Brandy won 31 CCs (25 with BOB), 20 RCCs, four Hound Groups, 2 Res Hound Groups, 2 Res BIS All Breed Championship shows, seven BIS Breed Championship shows, BOB at Crufts in 1988 and 1992, Beagle Association Winners' Contest and was also the Welsh Contest of Champions winner in 1992. He sired four Champions.

Ch. Dialynne Princess at Webline, born in 1986 (Sire Ch. Solomon of Dialynne, Dam Dicarl Get Going Of Dialynne). She was made up into a Champion by Mr. McInnes at the Ladies Kennel Club in 1987. In total, she won 12 CCs and a Best of Breed. Very popular, her beautiful head was commemorated on a special set of crockery and breed mementoes.

All-breed shows and Best in Show at the 1997 Hound Show. He was the top hound in the country in 1997 and by 1999 had sired six British Champions.

In 1993 Ch. Bayard Syndicat of Lowyck, owned by Colin and Pat Lomax, was Best of Breed at Crufts when she won the Hound Group. She was again BOB in 1994 and her 23rd CC was also won at Crufts in 2000 when she was a nine-year-old veteran.

At the end of the century the dominant kennel was still Dialynne, but the established kennels of Bayard (Jill Peak), Rossut (now owned by Catherine's daughter, Patricia), Raimex (Diana Brown), Newlin (Liz Calikes), and Dufosee (Veronica Bradley and Ken Burgess) continued to breed high-quality hounds.

Notable dogs during this period were: Ch. Soloman of Dialynne, Ch. Dialynne Pedlar, Ch. Dialynne Solison, Ch. Bayard The Cat's Pyjamas, Ch. Bayard Zachariah, Ch. Dufosee Nobility, Ch. Dufosee Influence, Ch. Bondlea Poet, Ch. Mistylaw Gentleman and Ch. Raimex Kracker. Notable bitches were: Ch. Dialynne Alice, Ch. Dialynne Princess of Webline, Ch. Norcis Foxy Lady, Ch. Bondlea Pebbles, Ch. Dufosee Penny Black, Ch. Dufosee Queen Bee, Ch. Fallowfield Dilly and Ch. Lowyck Kissin' Cousin.

THE 21st CENTURY

The early part of this century saw Dialynne's success continue with the kennel being run by Marion Spavin's family who produced 12 Champions in the first 10 years. The dog line was particularly strong with Champions Hallmark,

Ch & Ir. Ch. Serenaker Devil Woman, aka Charlie. (Rossut Navigator x Serenaker Carousel). Born in 2003. Charlie won 21 CCs, 12 RCCs, 15 BOB, two Group 2s, two Group 3s, and two Group 4s. She was top Beagle in 2006, also winning BOB and Hound Group 3 at Crufts. In the same year, she was also BOB and Hound Group winner at the St. Patrick's day show. Charlie was Top brood bitch 2007 and runner up in 2008. She has produced two Champion children, and another daughter followed in her pawprints by winning BOB and being short-listed in the final seven of the Hound Group at Crufts in 2011.
Photo: Dave Holmes.

Masterpiece and Maximus being noteworthy, the latter winning Best of Breed and the Hound Group at Crufts in 2008. The kennel imported Ch. Blackspot Entrepreneur from Argentina because of his Dialynne blood. Although her stud dog Ch. Fallowfield Douglas was producing Champions, Christine Lewis imported stock from the USA and Canada. Two well-known bitches from this kennel are Delilah and Darlene. Elizabeth Calikes' Newlin kennels became the top Beagle kennel in Scotland.

SIZE MATTERS

When Masters of Hounds were eager to maintain the standard of their packs, they paid considerable attention to the size of their hounds and, to a lesser degree, their colour. These two qualities also engaged the minds of those who bred their hounds for the show ring and have been constant subjects of discussion to the present day. Every few years the opinion has been expressed that Beagles were becoming too big, and in the 1960s Thelma Gray and Joan Beck made an attempt to reduce height by importing hounds from the USA.

There was no fixed height for hunting in Britain, but the Masters bred their hounds according to the type of country over which they were hunting. The smaller hounds were considered ideal for the flat ground, but more height was desirable over uneven and hilly ground. When The Beagle Club published its first Standard for the breed, it settled for the unusually wide range of 13 to 16 inches (33-40.6 cms) measured at the withers. This was later modified by the Kennel Club, which did not want hounds to be measured in the ring by introducing the word 'desirable'. This meant that judges need not disqualify hounds that exceeded the 13-16 ins limit but could penalise them. In the USA the maximum heights of 15 ins (38 cms) and 13 ins (33 cms) are rigid and hounds exceeding these limits are disqualified.

COLOURS AND MARKINGS

The many different colours and shades of colour displayed by the Beagle has been one of the reasons for its popularity. A few Masters went to considerable trouble to breed their packs to one particular colour, although it was accepted there was no difference in the performance of differently coloured hounds. Black, white and tan, known as tricolour, were the most popular. It was the same in the show ring for many years; tricolours were dominant and it was rare for a lemon and white or tan and white hound to win. Gradually, it was realised that some hounds of those colours possessed considerable quality, and judges started to favour them so much they were accused of having a colour bias.

It was also realised that the interpretation of the Breed Standard requirement of 'any recognised hound colour' was becoming more varied, as breeders became more and more remote from the hunting hounds of the 19th century. This was particularly so in countries such as Australia, New Zealand and South Africa where there was little hunting tradition. In 1980 moves were made by The Beagle Club to ask the Kennel Club to adopt a more precise description. Eventually, in 2010 the KC agreed to a request made by all the British breed clubs to include all the permissible colours in the Standard. Tricolours are still the most popular, but in the show ring all the approved colours have to be treated as equal.

AUSTRALIAN SHOW SCENE

In the early 1950s, showing Beagles started to become popular in Australia. The Serenata kennels, owned by Jess and Jim Wilmott, brought out two imports from the UK – Ch. Stanhurst Raleigh and Ch Derawuda Bellmaid – both contributing to the breed and show scene. The Bluebell kennels which campaigned Ch. Rosaval Kiwi, bred by Thelma Gray, and the Beagles that featured with President Johnson in the media on his visit from America helped to popularise the breed further.

Jill Kirk (nee Woods), owner of the Balihai kennels, purchased her first show Beagle back in 1958, and Jill is still winning today. She imported the American Champion, Elsy's King of Diamonds, and this signalled the start of Australians looking to other countries, rather than relying solely on England, for new stock. The Balihai kennel produced many winners including Ch. Bailihai Bacardi Rum and the Best in Show winner, Ch Balihai Tiki, owned by Ted and Maureen Edwards.

In the Seventies, Thelma Gray emigrated from England and her Rozavel Beagles were a force to be reckoned with in their new

Norma Shipley (pictured with medals) has been a highly successful breeder, and her Filnor bloodlines are well known in Australia. She bred or owned all the hounds pictured – they were all winners or placed at the Beagle National 2003 hosted by the Beagle Club of Victoria.

homeland. Nina Bieberitz, based in Victoria, put the tan and white Beagle on the map with Ch. Michlaine Topaz, although it is fair to say that, even today, tan and white Beagles struggle to take top awards as many of the all-round judges prefer their more flashy tricolour relations. Danny Scott (Scottholme) based in Sydney, New South Wales, made a big impression on the breed with Ch. Lees Pennon, imported from Pat Curties in the UK. This dog sired many Champions throughout Australia, and in 1964 he became the first recipient of the Australian National Beagle Council Award of Merit (AOM), given to outstanding representatives of the breed based on a strict criteria of show wins and/or the wins of their progeny. Also taken into account are Beagles that excelled at Obedience, Tracking or Agility.
Recipients include:

- 1968: Ch Bluebell Kiwi Son , owned by Nina Bieberitz
- 1969: Aust. and NZ Ch Annasline Fanfare (Imp. UK), owned by Danny Scott
- 1979: Ch Bonnymead Briar Rose, bred by Noreen Harris, owned by Barbara Martin.
- 1979: Aust. Am. Ch. Torbay Henrietta, bred by Lesley and David Hiltz
- 1979: Ch Manahound Match Point, bred by Liz Rosbach.

Norma Shipley, owner of the Filnor kennels in Queensland, proved to be a very clever breeder of Beagles starting from the 1980s to the current day. The Orabay kennels, also in Queensland, has produced Champions for many countries.

In Western Australia the Sligrachan kennels, owned by Marion Watson, is still breeding and exhibiting Champions in partnership with her daughter and granddaughter. The Bonnymead kennels, owned by Noreen Harris in Victoria, has combined the best of UK and American bloodlines to produce many Champions. Lesley and Brian Childs from NSW have made their stamp on the breed by importing from America, breeding locally, and then exporting a Best in Show winner to the UK. The Kislev kennels in Queensland is another small kennel which consistently breeds Champions and 'in-Show' winners throughout the country. At the present time, Beagles are well represented in the show ring in all states of Australia, with Western Australia, South Australia, Victoria, New South Wales and Queensland all having annual breed club (specialty) shows. In addition, each state capital has its own yearly Royal Agricultural Show (Royal), with Beagles being exhibited in good numbers. Most states also have specialty Hound Club Shows and, again, Beagles are well represented.

Aust. Ch. Braylodge St Nicholas, owned and bred by Barbara Martin.

Beagle Club of Victoria sire and progeny: Am. Can. NZ. Aust. Ch. Tradewinds Lil' Bit of Fire (*imp.* USA), owned by Brian and Lesley Childs (far left).

All Breed Championship Shows are held right throughout the year, and on any given weekend there is sure to be a Championship Show in each state. In fact, the larger states often have a number of shows held on the same day, often vast distances apart. Every three years one of the state Beagle clubs hosts a Beagle National, usually with an English judge presiding. These shows attract a large inter-state entry and are generally held over two or three days, enabling breeders/exhibitors who would never normally meet to get together and view each other's stock at first hand. Australia's top Beagles not only win at breed level, but are top contenders for Best In Group and often Best in Show All Breeds awards. The home bred Australian Grand Champion, Brialey Itn A Bit, is a multi Best In Show All Breeds winner, as were both his sire, Australian, New Zealand, American, Canadian Champion Tradewinds Lil' Bit Of Fire (imp. USA); and his dam, Australian

Grand Champion Moonmagik Rain Dancer. Some of the top performing dogs of recent years also include: Grand Champion Beagelee Finnish Spirit, Grand Champion Hilldamar Classic Rumour, and Grand Champion Clarion Cotton Bauble. Representing top winning bitches are: Australian Grand Champion Orobay Optical Magic, Ch. Nanguynah Spell At Kislev and Grand Champion Treeview American Design. Among the top winning kennels from yesteryear, Balihai, Clarion & Sligrachan are still breeding and winning today.

BEAGLES IN THE US
We are fortunate to have Lori Norman help us view the development of the Beagle in America. She has been showing Beagles since 1963, breeding them since 1970, and is an avid historian of the breed.

The American Beagle evolved into what we see today through the influence of many dogs and

breeders over the past 60 years. The contemporary Beagle began to take shape in the 1940s, when the Hess's beautiful dog, Ch. Duke Sinatra, and Sam Granata's Ch. Thornridge Wrinkles (sire of 76 Champions) showed that Beagles could be winning show dogs. The Beagle's evolution continued through the 1950s where we found dogs that starred in the ring and then left their marks through their progeny, for future generations. With breeders such as James Geddes (Geddesburg), Lee Wade (Kinsman), Arthur and Carroll Gordon (Page Mill), and Ed Jenner (Forest), we found pioneers and mentors for those yet to come.

THE SIXTIES
Ed Jenner's girl, Ch. Socum Tammy, won Best of Variety at Westminster in 1960, and showed that she could play with the big boys in the ring. She then went on to produce more than 12 Champions. Other stars of the

TOP PRODUCERS

The 1960s was prolific in its abundance of important dogs. However, the American Beagle world saw two giants in that decade. From them came most of the winners in the following decade, and the pedigrees of today's winning American dogs can be traced back to them.

The first was the Best In Show 15 ins dog, Ch. Wandering Wind, bred by Donna Rayburn, and owned by Arthur and Carroll Gordon (Page Mill), and later, by Dr. Anton and Judy Musladin (The Whim's). Windy sired 35 Champions in limited breeding, and was a grandson of Ch. Page Mill Downbeat. The other was Marcia Foy's 15 ins dog, Ch. King's Creek Triple Threat, bred by Michele (Mike) Leathers Billings of King's Creek Kennels. He sired 78 Champions and was among the Top Ten Beagles in the US for seven years (1965-1971). He won the first National Beagle Club of America National Specialty show in 1970.

Am. Ch. Wandering Wind (15 ins). 'Windy' was a multiple Group and Best In Show winner, with limited showing. Despite quite selected access to mates, he produced 35 Champions. Windy had the uncanny ability to sire offspring that themselves were notable producers, and appears in many pedigrees of today's winners. Bred by Donna Rayburn, and owned by Arthur and Carroll Gordon (Page Mill), he was later owned by Dr. Anton and Judy Musladin (The Whim's).

Am. Ch. King's Creek Triple Threat (15 ins). 'Trippe' won Best of Breed at the first National Beagle Club of America Specialty in 1970, at age seven. He won Best of Variety at Westminster four times, and placed in the Hound Group there once. A multiple Best In Show winner and Top-Producing Sire, he produced 78 Champions, including several Group/Specialty winning dogs. Two progeny became Number 1 Beagle in the Seventies. He was bred by Michelle (Mike) Leathers Billings (King's Creek), and owned by Marcia Foy (Foyscroft).
Photo: Schafer.

Fifties, frequently found in pedigrees of most of today's American Beagles, were Ch. Kinsman Jimmy Valentine, Ch. Gay Boy of Geddesburg, Ch. Page Mill Downbeat; and Hollis Wilson's Ch. End O'Maine's Ridge Runner. This dog was himself a son of Jimmy Valentine.

Among the notable events of the early 1960s was the merger of John and Jean Refieuna's Johjean line with Ed Jenner's Forest line. This merger continued through future generations under the Johjean name. They later brought us such winners as Ch. Johjean

Jubilation T. Cornball, who won the National Beagle Club of America's 1972 National Specialty. This dog's dam was Ch. Socum Tammy. They also gave us producers such as Ch. Johjean Bill Jamboree Jubal, the dam of 14 Champions *and* the foundation for Virginia Coleman's Colegren Beagles in the Sixties.

The 1960s saw numerous breeders make lasting contributions to the American Beagle. Dogs from these breeders are found in the backgrounds of most of today's winners: Alpha-Centauri, Busch,

Colegren, Fulmont, King's Creek, Starcrest, Validay, Wagon Wheel, White Acres, The Whims, and toward the end of the decade, Teloca (then called Robin's). These were but a few of the Beagle breeders who emerged from the decade leaving their marks on the breed.

THE SEVENTIES
The Seventies were dominated by offspring of Ch. Wandering Wind and Ch. King's Creek Triple Threat. Ch. The Whim's Buckeye, a 13-in dog bred and owned by Dr. Anton and Judy Musladin, was a son of

Am. Ch. Navan's Triple Trouble Rick (15 ins). 'Rick' won Best of Breed at the 1975 and 1976 National Beagle Club of America Specialty shows, Best of Variety at Westminster, and other Specialty Bests of Breed. A multiple Group and Best In Show winner, he produced 55 Champions, including Group and Best In Show winners, and other top-producing progeny. Rick was bred by Nancy Vanstrum Cannon (Navan), and co-owned by her and Virginia Flowers (Pixshire). Rick was handled by Virginia Flowers (pictured). *Photo: Earl Graham.*

Am. Ch. The Whim's Cock of the Walk (13 ins). This was America's Top Beagle for 1975, winning Specialties and Best In Show as did his sire, Ch. The Whim's Buckeye. Himself the sire of 42 Champions, he was bred and owned by Judy Musladin, (The Whim's), and handled by Marvin Cates. *Photo: Jayne Langdon.*

Wandering Wind. The Musladins also gave us 13 ins Ch. The Whim's Cock of the Walk, a Buckeye son, and a top winner and top producer in his own right.

Ch. Navan's Triple Trouble Rick, was a 15 ins son of Triple Threat, bred by Nancy Vanstrum Cannon (Navan) and co-owned by her and Virginia Flowers. William and Cecile Busch's 15 ins Wandering Wind grandson, Ch. Busch's Nuts To You of Brendon, co-owned by them and Brenda Gentry, became the foundation for their successful Busch line of Beagles. Anna Katherine Nicholas' 15 ins dog, Ch. Rockaplenty's Wild Oats, aka Tuffy, bred by Carroll Gordon Diaz, was a Triple Threat son and a grandson of Ch. Wandering Wind. Tuffy was the first high profile dog to combine the pedigrees of Triple Threat (East coast) and Wandering Wind (West coast).

The Seventies also brought us some breeders who built upon strengths of the past to help shape the breed's future in America. The decade introduced us to Chardon, Starbuck (later to become Starbuck-Torbay), Navan, Bedlam, Merry Song, Pin Oaks, Plain & Fancy, Swan Lake, Lokavi, Whiskey Creek, Timberlost, Pixshire, Junior's, Chrisette, SureLuv, and more. As the breed became increasingly more popular in the show ring, the number of breeders correspondingly expanded.

To this day, still holding the record for top-producing American Beagle sire of all-time is 15 ins Ch. Starbuck's Hang 'Em High. He was sired by The Whim's Buckeye, bred by David L. Hiltz. From these dogs came the American winners for the 1980s.

Am. Ch. SureLuv's Heather Mist (15 ins).
'Heather' was not only a prolific producer with 16 Champions to her credit, but many of these became top producers as well. Among her 16 progeny are two Best In Show dogs. Dam of the Year in 1983, she provided the foundation for many of today's successful breeders. Her daughter, Ch. SureLuv's Summer Mist of Harnett, remains the Top-Producing Dam of all-time, with 23 Champions. Her sons have produced over 120 Champions. Heather was bred and owned by Helen Daley Hemby (SureLuv). *Photo: Helen Daley Hemby.*

Am. Ch. Teloca Patches Littl' Dickens (13ins).
'Dickens' sired 105 Champions, and still holds the all-breed record for most Champions produced in one year, with 39! A two-time winner of the National Beagle Club of America Specialty; a four-time Variety winner at Westminster resulting in three Group placements, 13 All Breed Best in Shows, Top Beagle in the US for two years. He also was the Top Sire among all breeds, two years running. Bred by Charles Grant (Patches) and Marie Shuart (Teloca), he was handled by Wade Burns and owned by Wade and Jon Woodring (Lanbur). Dickens became the foundation of their bloodline. *Photo: Earl Graham.*

Am. Ch. Lanbur's Miss Fleetwood (13 ins).
'Judy's' wins include 40 all-breed Bests In Show, 120 Group Firsts, three National Beagle Club of America Bests of Breed (including one from the Veterans class), four Westminster Bests of Variety and three consecutive Westminster Group Placements. She is the dam of 11 Champions, including Ch. Lanbur The Continental. Bred by Wade Burns and Jon Woodring (Lanbur), Judy was owned by Eddie Dziuk, Wade, Jon, and Jeffrey Slatkin.
Photo: Kohler

Am. Ch. Lanbur The Continental (13 ins).
'Lincoln' is the son of Ch. Lanbur's Miss Fleetwood. He sired 82 Champions, including five different Best In Show winners. He was bred and owned by Wade Burns, John Woodring, and Eddie Dziuk (Lanbur).
Photo: Jon Woodring

THE EIGHTIES

The 1980s introduced one bitch that left quite an imprint on our American Beagles. Helen Daley Hemby's (SureLuv) 15 ins Ch. SureLuv's Heather Mist was a daughter of Ch. Navan's Triple Trouble Rick, and was the National Beagle Club of America's Top-Producing Dam of 1983. Her mother is a granddaughter of Ch. King's Creek Triple Threat, and brings Ch. Duke Sinatra into the pedigree. She seemed to be a compilation of many prolific dogs of the past. She herself produced 16 Champions. However, of those 16, there were several top winning and top producing dogs and bitches, not the least of which were her daughter, Ch. SureLuv's

Sumer Mist of Harnett, who holds the record for the top-producing dam of all-time (with 23); and Ch. SureLuv Fran-Ray's Bandit who produced 70 Champions.

Jon Woodring and Wade Burns' (Lanbur) 13 ins dog, Ch. Teloca Patches Littl' Dickens, bred by Charles Grant, and Marie Shuart (Teloca), brings together the lines of Ch. King's Creek Triple Threat and Ch. Wandering Wind through Ch. The Whim's Buckeye. It is this dog that propelled Wade Burns and Jon Woodring (Lanbur) into prominence in America. This dog still holds the record for siring the most Champions in a one-year period – 39! He sired 105 Champions overall, notably Ch. SureLuv Fran-Ray's Bandit out of

Ch. SureLuv's Heather Mist. This began a long tradition of success for Lanbur.

In the late 1980s Ch. SureLuv Fran-Ray's Bandit sired Ch. Lanbur The Company Car, co-owned by Eddie Dziuk, Wade Burns, and Jon Woodring (Lanbur). He was Number One Beagle, a National Specialty winner, and produced 35 Champions. Among them were Ch. Lanbur Miss Fleetwood, a Best In Show and multi-Specialty Best of Breed winner, and Ch. Lanbur Coupe de Ville, who produced 78 Champions in the 1990s. Ch. Lanbur Miss Fleetwood, co-owned by Wade Burns, Jon Woodring and Eddie Dziuk (Lanbur), went on to

Am. Ch. Shaw's Spirit of the Chase (15 ins).
'Chase' started his career at 8½ months with Winners Dog, Best of Winners and Best Puppy at the 1994 National Beagle Club Specialty. He is a Group and Specialty winner, with two National Beagle Club of America Awards Of Merit. Chase won Best of Breed at the 2005 Phoenix Beagle Club Specialty and Best Veteran In Show and an Award Of Merit at the 2005 National Beagle Club of America Specialty at age 12! He is the sire of 95 Champions and was the Top-Producing Sire in 1997 and 1998. Chase was bred and owned by John and Peggy Shaw (Shaw's).

Photo: Andrew Brace.

Am.Ch. Lanbur Carson City (13 ins).
'Carson' has won three Bests In Show and several Groups. His greatest asset is in his progeny. Carson has produced 35 Champions as of this writing. That number will increase as more of his offspring enter the show ring. He was bred and owned by Eddie Dziuk, Wade Burns, and Jon Woodring (Lanbur) and handled by Jon or Eddie.

Photo: Baines.

produce Ch. Lanbur The Continental in the early 1990s. The Continental was the sire of five different Best in Show winners and 82 Champions.

THE NINETIES
In the 1990s, Ch. Shaw's Spirit of the Chase, owned by John and Peggy Shaw, brought together Ch. Starbuck's Hang 'em High, Ch. Navan's Triple Trouble Rick, and Ch. Busch's Nuts To You of Brendon. He was a Group and Specialty-winning dog who sired 95 Champions. At 12 years old, he won a Specialty Best n Show from the Veteran Class. He sired 13 ins Ch. Kahootz Chase Manhattan, who went on to sire 70 Champions. Among those

Champions is 13 ins Ch. Kowtown High Speed Chase, a contemporary multiple Best in Show and Specialty winner, who is also proving to be a top producer.

THE CURRENT SCENE
Today's breeders, aside from those mentioned earlier, include Windkist, Torqay, Bayou Oaks, Shaw, Roirdan, K-Run, Just-Wright, RK N'Tooker, Skyline, Springfield, Saranan, Merry Song, Vinla, Albedo, Rockwood, Copper Rose, Barrister, Tesoros, Kowtown, Aladar, Wishing Well, Encore, Scentini, Danter, Ha-Penny, Meadowcrest, Alamo, Cabaret, Magnolia, Irish Coffee, Wilkeep, Meadowland, Honey Pot, Talbot Hill, Jabrwoki, Beowulf, Milroc,

Durrisdeer, We-Fuss, and many more. They are the trusted stewards of the breed in America today. The future of the American Beagle will be forged in their hands.

Today's American Beagle has been shaped by the past, but is carried forward by the winners and producers of this millennium. Ch. Lanbur's Carson City, Ch. Springfield'N'Skylines Big Shot, Ch. Windkist A Walk In the Park, and Ch. Ha-Penny's Too Much Trouble, are just a few of today's winners proving their merits as producers. New dogs will replace these in the coming years, but consistently we will find that somewhere in their pedigrees those old familiar names live on.

A BEAGLE FOR YOUR LIFESTYLE

Chapter 3

The Beagle is the smallest scent hound, bred to be kept and worked in a pack. This is a dog that has many attributes that have been 'bred in' for hundreds of years, so when deciding to have a Beagle as a family pet, we must be aware of how these features will impact on both the hound's and our own lifestyles.

The term 'scent hound' tells us that the Beagle was used to hunt by scent, so from an early age he senses the world around him by reading the smells that his nose receives. In reality, this means that when the nose is working, he is using his ears and his sight to a lesser extent. This may give the impression to a new owner that their Beagle is not listening or looking at them, and is being stubborn and disinterested.

Owners that have had experience keeping other breeds struggle with this seemingly non-reactive nature. However, different breeds react to training techniques in different ways depending on their original purpose. For example, herding breeds, like Border Collies, use their ears and eyes more intently, as they were bred to stare at the flock and listen to the shepherd's instructions. The Beagle has a single purpose in that he has to follow a scent, so even if a hare appears in front of him, he must not take any notice of it, but must follow its scent to that point.

The most common 'urban myth' question asked by new owners is: "Will he come back if I let him off his lead?" My answer is: "Yes, if you speak Beagle." When entering new areas the Beagle will try to 'read' the area

by finding scents. If he is off his lead, he will run around the area, trying to find interesting smells to follow. He also expects that you will, as a member of his pack, want to join him on the trail. So when he finds a good scent, he will glance back for a second to see if you are coming, too. It is at this point that you must show him that this is not what you are going to do, and actually turn and walk in the opposite direction. For new owners, this is a brave thing to do, but the result will be that the pack instinct kicks in and your Beagle should join you on your chosen path – well, that's the theory!

BEAGLE BASICS

The fact that the Beagle is a small pack hound has left us with a lot of positive attributes that suit him well to a family life. He has been

IS A BEAGLE RIGHT FOR YOU?

Will my Beagle come back if I let him off the lead?

The Beagle is highly sociable and enjoys company – both human and canine.

Do you have the time and the energy to devote to a Beagle puppy?

bred to be a highly social animal, and the desire to belong to a pack is strong. However, I do not advise getting two puppies at the same time, as you would never be able to train them in unison.

A Beagle's nature should be easygoing and non-aggressive. Pack hounds have to get on with each other, with everyone knowing their place, so a Beagle needs company and interaction, especially when young, whether it is human or canine. You and your family are seen as the pack he now belongs to; he is certainly not a 'home alone' dog.

This breed is small enough to sit on your lap, but sturdy enough to go on long country walks. The Beagle is built on the basic dog pattern with no deformities to hamper his function. He is a no-nonsense dog, but will still enjoy being fussed and taking part in games with the children. The short coat means easy cleaning and little grooming, but he does shed, so be aware when wearing dark-coloured clothes.

Briefly, the Beagle is a small, short-coated, sweet-natured hound that loves people and can be equally at home on your sofa or enjoying brisk walks. He should be fit and healthy, so some consideration must be given to his diet and exercise. A Beagle does very well on most foods but, unfortunately, this can lead to

The breeder will be anxious to find the best homes possible for the puppies.

weight gain, so it is about balancing the diet and amount of exercise he is given.

If your family are couch potatoes, don't get a Beagle! Equally, if you ask your dog to run a marathon every day, he will not take kindly to cutting back on that level of exercise if you are ill or busy doing other things. When caring for a dog of any breed, routine and structure are important; a stable family makes for a stable, well-balanced Beagle. The Beagle is a big hound in a small frame, so do not expect him to sit like an ornament at your feet; he is a bouncy, fun-loving character that needs to interact with people and cannot be switched on and off like a toy.

CAN YOU COPE WITH A PUPPY?

Looking for the puppy to suit you and your lifestyle and doing the necessary research is fundamental to the successful relationship that you will, hopefully, build with your new pup. You need to assess your family and home life and work out what you can offer a Beagle puppy. For example, how old are your children (if you have them)? Do they need as much interaction and support as the puppy will, or are they slightly older and more independent and able to take on a responsible role in the puppy's life?

The time commitment involved in taking on a puppy is huge, and although nobody is at home every hour of the day, someone must be available for large portions of the day, every day. If you work from home, that is ideal, but you must still find the time to engage and interact with your puppy.

In general, the Beagle is a hardy breed, but medical costs must be planned for. Of course, you can take out insurance, but be aware that routine and preventative health care is not covered. The basic puppy kit, including food and equipment (brushes, bowls, leads, crates, bedding, etc.) is expensive. You may also need to pay boarding fees if you need the services of kennels when you go away on holiday, or you may need to pay a dog-sitter if you are away

Are all the family committed to taking on a Beagle?

Photo © istockphoto.com/Sadeugra.

from home for lengthy periods.

You also need to look at your home and garden from a puppy's perspective and work out what changes you will need to make in order to provide an environment that is safe and secure. Indoors, a room with washable floors and no family antiques will help; outdoors, a secure fence and a safe place to use as a toilet are essential.

If you have assessed correctly and have a clear picture of how your new puppy will fit into your family's lifestyle, it means there should be fewer shocks or surprises for both of you. A responsible breeder will also help you in this process, as he is just as eager as you to get the right home for his precious puppy. Be prepared to be asked personal questions about your family and home life, and answer them as

honestly as you can. Giving up a puppy to be rehomed because you got it wrong is a worst-case scenario – so let's try to get it right the first time!

GREAT EXPECTATIONS

When you are thinking about taking on a puppy, you probably have a lovely picture in your mind of how it will be: the new puppy cuddled up in your lap, playing happily with the children, romping through summer meadows, everything going well and all is trouble-free…

Of course, that is how we would all like it to be, but it is not a matter of chance; research is the key. My first question to new owners is: "Why do you a want a Beagle?" I then ask: "How many Beagles have you met?" Practical experience of Beagle owners is very valuable as is 'hands on'

Beagle experience – i.e. what does a Beagle feel and smell like? How does it feel to have one on your knee?

Very often, potential owners find that when they visit adult Beagles and experience taking them for a walk and interacting with them, many questions emerge that they probably would not have considered had they just looked at a litter of puppies. Responsible breeders should encourage this practice. Contact your national kennel club for details of breeders and clubs in your area; your local vet may be able to put you in touch with other owners, too, as practices usually run puppy socialisation classes.

The whole family must be united in wanting a puppy and agree on a joint strategy so the puppy gets consistent treatment and handling. In the first few weeks, a controlled environment is vitally important so that a puppy leans what is expected of him and settles into his new home.

Play with children should be supervised, as some forms of play can encourage nipping. Although nipping and mouthing are natural between littermates, it is not appropriate with people, and the puppy must learn to inhibit these behaviours. Children also need to understand that puppies play hard and sleep hard; quiet time is important, so letting the puppy sleep is not open to negotiation.

The motto for training is "early and often" – it is never too early to start, and lessons will need to be repeated often so a puppy understands what is required. However, make sure that training is kept simple and is always enjoyable. Although you can generalise about breed characteristics, individual traits within each hound can vary and so your puppy could be more motivated by play while others are food driven. It is your job to find out what works for a Beagle, and what works for your individual puppy.

DOG OR BITCH?

The essence of a pack is centred on uniformity in size, colour and balance of sexes, therefore the difference in the sexes and their characteristics is less marked in Beagles than in other breeds. The development of male dogs is similar to that of humans in that females develop slightly quicker

intellectually, their perception and memory putting them forward in the problem-solving stakes. Males tend to be more dependent and unsure about new situations, or they see no danger and blunder into new activities and situations.

This is usually a shock to people who have heard that bitches are more loving and gentle, when, in fact, they are usually the head of the escape committee and can be little madams that do not want to be petted. Male hounds are generally big soppy lumps that need lots of support.

Sexual maturity brings the

differences between the sexes into sharp focus and the question of having a bitch in season or a dog who is constantly looking for sexual interest is one that each family must decide. Beagle males will show an interest in female scents all the time, although this fades with age, while a bitch shows sexual interest only while 'in season'.

The option of neutering always brings out our human emotions – men are reluctant to have their male counterpart castrated and women often think that a litter could be a fulfilling experience for both the mother dog and the

The male (left) looks for support from his human family, whereas the female (right) tends to be more independent.

family. The best plan is to seek advice from a vet and discuss what options are available, and the recommended age for surgery.

Choosing the sex of your puppy is a personal decision, but seek advice from the breeder, other owners and, of course, your vet.

COAT AND COLOUR

There are potentially 22 colour combinations in the breed, but the most common colour is tricolour (black, tan and white) followed by tan and white, and the slightly less common lemon and white.

A blanketed tri is the colour most commonly requested by new owners. This takes the form of a tan hound with white muzzle, blaze, throat, chest, legs and tip of tail with a blanket or saddle of black across their back. Brightly marked or flashy tris have more white, such as a white collar or a half-white tail. The term 'broken tri' really confuses people; it refers to the tri pattern being broken up into patches (not that the hound is damaged in some way). Many breeders use the term 'open marked tri', which is less confusing.

Beagle puppies that will eventually be tricolour are actually born black and white. The tan

A blanketed tricolour has a distinctive black 'saddle'.

comes through slowly, the white areas will shrink, and so a very thin or narrow blaze may disappear completely. Tan and whites and lemons are born almost white, depending on the shade of the adult colour. Again, they can be more covered or open marked.

Mottled hounds are also seen in the ring. The gene is similar to the roan gene in Cocker Spaniels and converts any colour to a heavily spotted pattern, often giving a blue look to the hound.

Pieds, pure whites or black and whites are very rare; hare pieds give the impression of the colour of the hare and are caused by the sable gene. The only black and whites I have seen were, in fact, true tricolours, as they had rich

tan spots above each eye, on the cheeks and under the tail, rather like the tricolour example found in spaniels. The only colour not recognised is a liver or chocolate tri.

FINDING A BREEDER

Novice owners have a great challenge in trying to find a reputable breeder. The first contact for any pedigree puppy should be the organisation that controls and monitors the practice of breeding pedigree dogs, i.e. the national kennel club. If you go to the website, you will find breed information as well as contact details for breed clubs and breeders. Most breed clubs also have websites with a great wealth of breed-specific advice, as well as information on litters available bred by club members. Breed club members will be bound by a code of conduct, and so support and guidance should be available to you for the lifetime of the hound.

The difficulty with searching for a puppy outside of these organisations is that, basically, anyone can be a breeder. It is all too easy to see a photo of a puppy in a less than satisfactory environment and then feel you must buy the pup to save him from further distress. This never has a happy ending. Even if the puppy survives the life-long consequences of poor nutrition, indiscriminate breeding, bad socialisation, poor sanitary conditions and premature removal from his mother, these factors will always have an effect on his behaviour, his appearance when adult, his health – and your bank balance!

Pedigree dogs should not be bred for profit; a breeder's primary concern should be to carry on a line of healthy, typical dogs. A reputable breeder should be able to provide you with evidence of their previous good practice, and you should also find out how they intend to conduct the purchase, the choice of puppy and after-sales support they offer.

Puppy farmers and puppy dealers are very clever at confusing the issue by dragging pups in from a barn and setting them on the sofa for a 'home reared' photo. Then, when you visit the premises, you are shown to a room and find 'the one you can have' ready for you. So take your time and do not go for the first puppy you see. If you are not sure about something, take a step back and do some research or ask more questions.

The internet is a valuable tool

You need to find a breeder who has a reputation for producing sound, healthy puppies that are typical of the breed.

for instant information, but a reputable breeder would not conduct a sale online. Breeders' websites are a good starting point but, again, you will need to make several visits and ask a lot of questions before a purchase is made. Bear in mind, the top breeders often have a waiting list, but it is worth waiting to get the puppy you want.

VISITING A BREEDER
Finally, you have tracked down a breeder and have arranged a visit. What should you expect?

• Make a list of all the questions you want to ask, and make sure

you have plenty of time to discuss important issues in detail.
• Prepare to answer lots of questions yourself. A responsible breeder will want to find out about your lifestyle to see if you can offer a suitable home to one of their precious pups.
• Ask if you can see adult dogs who are closely related to the puppies, so you can get an idea of the type of dogs being produced and their temperament.
• Make sure you see the dam of the puppies. The pups may be weaned, so it can be difficult seeing her interacting with them, but you should ask if it is possible.
• It is unlikely that the sire will live on the premises, as breeders often travel long distances to find the perfect match for a bitch. However, you should be able to see a photo, a pedigree, and be given details of his show record.
• When you see the puppies, you need to assess the environment to ensure they have been reared in clean, hygienic conditions. You also need to find out how often they have been handled and socialised with people.

I have mixed feelings about children coming on the initial visit – often they want the puppy there and then, which puts too much

It is important to see the puppies with their mother as this will give you an idea of the temperament they are likely to inherit.

pressure on their parents. However, as a breeder, it gives me a chance to assess how responsible they are, and how much they know about looking after a puppy.

TYPE AND TEMPERAMENT
A good, healthy Beagle puppy should appear well fed and happy; a degree of 'plumpness' is desirable - a small body on firm, thick legs. The overall impression should be that the puppy has a little bit more of everything than he should have when he reaches maturity, so this means longer ears, bigger feet, more loose skin

and a head that rather looks like a St. Bernard! In fact, lots to grow into.

The tails should all be up and wagging, and puppies should come forward to greet you, showing no signs of hand shyness or stress at being touched. They should welcome being picked up and remain relaxed in your arms. A puppy that panics or freezes when held is not a good prospect for a family pet. If the pup is gently cradled on his back, he should not struggle. If he does, he is probably going to have a more dominant disposition. The puppy shivering in the corner is not

going to be a social hound either!

Puppies do play fight and try to establish pack order, so do not worry if your choice suddenly asserts himself with one of his littermates. However, the 'dispute' should be over and forgotten quickly, with no damage inflicted on either side.

HEALTH ALERT
The appearance of a healthy puppy should be chunky but not grossly fat; a puppy with a huge distended abdomen may have an infestation of worms. Ask the breeder about the litter's worming history and, at the same time,

check out the overall health record of the puppy's parents. The puppy should have no discharge from its eyes or ears and should appear lively and alert.

In Beagles there are a few congenital problems, such as steroid responsive meningitis, epilepsy and hip dysplasia, that do occur, but they are rare. In general, there are no routine health tests required by the Kennel Club so, in reality, the breed is free from major health issues.

For information on breed-specific conditions, see Chapter Eight: Happy and Healthy.

A SHOW PUPPY

Top show kennels have many years of experience when it comes to choosing their next Champion, but it is very difficult to guarantee that any puppy aged eight or ten weeks old will make it into the show ring and be successful Most breeders will only state that the puppy they are selling you is "promising". The only certain way to buy a show prospect is to go on a list and wait till the breeder has retained a couple of puppies from a litter, reared them correctly, trained them for the ring, made sure their adult dentition is correct and, ideally, taken them to a show and won with them. The breeder may let one go at this point – but you must expect to pay for all that hard work!

You can still buy a promising puppy and take the risk, but make sure the show kennel you go to has a record of selling good puppies that win for others. You must like their type of Beagle and take their advice, as most breeders only want the best representatives of their kennel to enter the ring. Hopefully, the breeder will take the time to go through the points of the puppy, explaining where the pup excels in relation to the Breed Standard, and will outline the techniques involved in rearing a show puppy, which are slightly different to rearing a companion. The list of dos and don'ts is large, so keep in contact with the breeder and follow his advice.

The breeder will help you to assess which puppy has show potential.

BOOKING A PUPPY

After talking to the breeder and looking at the puppies and their close relatives, you are now ready to make a decision and pick a puppy.

It may well be that the breeder has pick of the litter, or some of the pups may already be booked. This is rarely a problem, unless you are specifically looking for a show puppy, but make sure you are happy with the choice that is available before you select a puppy and pay a deposit.

Beagles are a breed that change colour rapidly from birth until the age they go to their new homes, which should be after seven weeks and generally eight or nine weeks. It can therefore be quite confusing trying to recognise your puppy in the tribe of bouncing babies. I try to find a marking that is specific to a particular puppy, and will not change much with age; I even take a photo so that the new owner and I are clear which puppy they have booked.

The breeder should make it clear if there are any conditions – such as restrictions on breeding or showing – attached to the sale, and these should be part of a contract. You should also be provided with a list of equipment you will need when your puppy comes home, and a diet sheet giving detailed information on the type of food and feeding regime required from puppyhood to adulthood.

The breeder will also give you details of the worming programme to date, flea treatment, and will advise you when vaccinations are due, although this should be confirmed with the vet in your area.

TAKING ON AN OLDER DOG

The charm of puppies is so appealing that most people do not consider the slightly older young adult or a retired show dog. However, there can be many positives in choosing a well-socialised, partially trained and possibly toilet-trained Beagle. For one thing, the Beagle you are buying is the finished product, and if he has gone beyond the teething phase, you should avoid chewing and other destructive behaviour.

Breeders may let a promising puppy go if he has developed a slight fault that makes him unsuitable for the show ring. In this situation, finding the right home is the most important factor. This type of hound has been well reared and well socialised, and usually has a lovely nature. Or it could be that the breeder has an older dog that has been retired from the ring or from breeding and needs the one-on-one attention that family life brings. Generally, an older Beagle will only need a few weeks of basic routine to settle into a forever home, so please consider this option if you feel you cannot cope with a puppy.

In some cases, the breeder may be prepared to sell an older dog.

RESCUED DOGS

Specialist rescue societies have a great track record in matching and placing Beagles in the right homes – and this is the key to successful rehoming. Be prepared to fill out a questionnaire about your home, your family and your lifestyle, which will facilitate a good match. However, the most vital piece of the puzzle is to try to discover the true history of the rescued dog. Finding out about his previous life, and as much about his temperament as possible, will help you to discover what his needs are and if you are able to fulfil them. For example, a young bouncy hound will fit in with a family with children, whereas an older, more sedate, hound may appreciate living with a retired couple.

Most rescue societies will allow you a trial period and will be on hand with back-up advice and support during the vital settling-in period.

THE PERFECT FAMILY PET

If you have taken on a Beagle puppy, he will gradually show his personality. A family pet will add enormously to your family and your Beagle should be able to take part in most aspects of your life in a positive way. As a dog owner, you must take responsibility for your puppy's socialisation and training, and also understand the impact that a badly trained, antisocial pet can have, not only in your home but also in the wider community.

Your Beagle should be trained to basic standards at the very least;

The Beagle thrives in a home where he respects his human family.

the puppy crèche or socialisation class comes in very useful, and later on you can take him to a Good Citizen training class where he can learn to be a well-trained, well-mannered hound that you can be proud of.

The easy maintenance with regard to grooming and cleaning means the Beagle is a 'go anywhere, do anything' dog, but because he is bred to hunt, he will also be able to find that dead seagull or fox faeces… To him, these smells are like the most expensive perfume and he will proceed to roll in them joyfully!

The main plus of the Beagle is

his friendly, outgoing nature and the strong desire to be part of your pack, which few breeds can match. If we add the easy maintenance and excellent health record, we have a small hound that should fit into most families. However, owners should be aware of the exercise needs of these little hunting dogs and the consequences of over-feeding and under-exercising. This is a breed that will give you and your family a very special kind of love and companionship, and your lives will undoubtedly be the richer for allowing a Beagle into your home.

THE NEW ARRIVAL

Chapter

efore you collect your new puppy, it is best to be well prepared and have your house, garden and family organised. Beagles are lively, inquisitive hounds and will soon explore their new surroundings, testing every boundary and challenging all the rules!

IN THE GARDEN

Beagles love to dig and chew, and Beagle puppies will try to eat almost anything. If you have precious or dangerous plants (there are detailed lists of dangerous plants on the internet), do fence them off or move them to a safe place.

Slug pellets and other harmful garden chemicals or materials must be stored securely, and make sure you do not use them anywhere where your Beagle can gain access, even if it might be accidental. Be careful of cocoa mulch; it contains an ingredient that smells like chocolate and attracts dogs. However, if consumed, a dog will become very ill and may even die.

Ponds are not such a problem when your Beagle is older but will need to be fenced off while he is a puppy. A pup must never be unsupervised by ponds or swimming pools.

Be aware that snails can cause lungworm in dogs if they are eaten (see page 137).

SECURITY

Your garden should be securely fenced. Plan for when your Beagle is fully grown as well as when he is tiny. If you are proud of your garden, consider fencing areas off so that you have areas where your Beagle will be free to play and enjoy himself. A Beagle loves to run and dig, so it is much easier to plan in advance in order to save problems later.

Things to consider:
- If you have hedges, are they lined with strong wire or fencing? If you have walls, are they tall enough to stop a Beagle jumping out or do they need wire on top?
- If you have wooden fencing, are there any weak areas that need a bit of work?
- Check that fences are secure at ground level – Beagles love digging.
- Are all boundaries secure at puppy height? Do your gates have gaps in them or under them that are large enough for a puppy to squeeze through?

If you spot any flaws in your boundary fencing, try to carry out the work that is required before your Beagle arrives. If your puppy

INTREPID EXPLORERS

Beagle puppies are on a mission to investigate everything they come across,
so make sure your garden is safe and secure.

discovers he can escape once, he will try to do it again and again – a Beagle can be very persistent.

If callers have access to areas where your Beagle will be left, consider putting up signs or install locks or catches that will stop visitors leaving gates open.

Beagle can be very fond of fruit and vegetables – mine have eaten all sorts, even the gooseberries and potatoes – so if you have a fruit and vegetable patch, you might like to fence it off, too.

Your puppy will need a place when he can rest undisturbed.

IN THE HOUSE

Firstly, decide where your Beagle will be allowed in the house. Will he be allowed in the bedrooms, will you let him sleep on the family sofas and chairs or will you restrict his access? It is very important that you decide on this before your new puppy arrives, as once he has discovered the delights of sleeping in your bed and on the best sofa, it will be very hard to stop him when he is older. What is cute and funny in a puppy is often very annoying in an adult Beagle, so think before you fall for those lovely, brown eyes…

Remember that your puppy will be teething and will want to chew anything that will help his teeth to come through. If you are a family that has shoes and toys everywhere, you will need to think about how you are going to keep them out of the puppy's way. Training everyone to tidy up their things can be a chore, but it saves upset and money.

In the same vein, if you give the puppy old shoes to chew, he will probably assume that all shoes are his. You will therefore need to provide chews and toys that he is allowed – and keep everything else out of his way. As time goes on, the chewing will reduce, but even older Beagles have their moments (often to get attention) and can revert to chewing.

Plan where your Beagle is going to sleep. Choose a quiet area where he can settle down without being disturbed. If you are using a crate, it can be in a corner of a room with newspapers on one half and his blanket in the other half. If you choose to use a bed, it is better to use a utility room or similar, that has a tiled floor where your puppy can be safely left.

Beagles are sociable dogs and like to be involved with the family action, but you will need to control your puppy's access to parts of the house. It pays to invest in a dog gate so that you can keep him out of mischief, but he can see you and know that you have not left him alone.

As with the garden, check for hazards and things a puppy could damage.

• Tidy away trailing flexes and electronic cables. Many a household has lost its internet connection thanks to a chewing puppy. Sadly, some puppies have died from chewing live electrical cables, so put wires behind covers or high enough to be out of reach.

• Find a safe place for remote controls and mobile phones – a common casualty to Beagle teeth! Remember that batteries are toxic if chewed. Move ornaments and other precious items. If you enjoy DIY, sewing, knitting or other crafts, keep your materials and equipment in a safe, Beagle-free area.

• Move plants to a safe place and, as for the garden, do check on any that are harmful to dogs. Most Beagles are very food-focused and will find any way of getting to extra supplies. Waste bins should be in cupboards or

An adult Beagle will still be happy to use a crate.

put above Beagle height, and food should be stored in closed cupboards. Dishwashers are a favourite target. Do not leave your dishwasher unattended when filling it or your Beagle will make a start on cleaning before you get a chance to switch it on!

- Do not assume everything you can eat will also be good for your Beagle. Some foods, including dark chocolate and raisins, can be dangerous, so check out the internet for lists of human food that are dangerous to dogs.
- Beware of air fresheners, carpet fresheners and biological detergents. Beagles can have sensitive skin and these products can cause severe itching or worse. Keep hazardous materials in locked cupboards, or make sure they are well out of reach.

BUYING EQUIPMENT

Keep equipment simple at the beginning. There are so many pet products on the market that it is easy to get carried away and buy things that you will never use.

BEDS

Dog beds come in many styles and sizes. Choose a solid plastic, middle-sized bed that your puppy will grow into. It is easy to buy one to fit a small puppy and find he's too big for it in just a few weeks.

A metal crate is ideal for a puppy as a first bed. Line it with some cosy bedding and, perhaps, cover it with a blanket, to provide a warm, safe place for your puppy to sleep. He can be left in it safely at night, at times when you are busy with things that Beagles should not get involved with, and while you are out of the house for short periods.

Choose a metal crate (soft ones are not fully secure). The smallest size that is suitable for a Beagle is around 60 cms x 46 cms x 54 cms (23.5 x 18 x 21 ins), which can also be used for travelling in the car. However, if you have the space in the house, a larger crate – 80 cm x 54 cm x 60 cm (31.5 x 21 x 23.5 ins) – gives more space to accommodate bedding at one end and newspaper at the other for when your puppy has to be left. A range of crates is available via the internet as well as in pet shops. Choose a solidly built crate with door catches that will not be easy for a Beagle to open.

BEDDING

Before your puppy comes home, buy a couple of dog blankets so that one can be used while one is washed. The best type to buy is synthetic fleece bedding, which is easy to wash and dry. Hopefully your puppy will come home with his own blanket from the breeder, which will have smells of his mother and home on it, to help him settle in. Try to use non-biological washing products for your Beagle's bedding and towels, as they are kinder to the skin and cause less irritation.

BOWLS AND FOOD
Medium-sized metal bowls are best. Buy two – one for water and one for food. The breeder should give you details of the food your puppy has been getting and will usually give you a starter pack of food. You may want to buy some treats for your puppy. The best type to buy are plain ones, like gravy bone biscuits, marrowbone biscuits or dried fish or beef jerky, but remember to subtract them from your Beagle's daily food allowance. It is all too easy for a Beagle to pile on the pounds and become unfit and prone to health problems. If you want to buy some chews, I suggest smaller rolled-hide ones, which are easier for their jaws when they are tiny.

For information on diet, see Chapter Five: The Best of Care.

DOG GATES
These are useful to restrict access to stairs, front doors and best rooms.

A gate can be used to restrict access to 'no go' areas in the house.

COLLAR
Initially, buy a small, soft puppy collar so that your puppy can get used to wearing it before he starts to go out on the lead. These are often sold with a small puppy lead.

Once your puppy has completed his vaccinations and can go out for walks, choose a strong collar, around 2 cms (¾ inch) wide, which can be adjusted as your puppy grows. There are a huge range of collars on the market today. The best choice is a collar that will take the strain of an active hound. Many collars are of synthetic material with a plastic clip, which do not stand up to hard

wear. If you buy one of these, make sure the clip is very strong and has a safety device in case the plastic clip breaks. Some collars are very cheaply made and will break if put under strain. Sadly, this has resulted in a few young Beagles being killed on the road. A buckle fastener is often the most secure.

Check the fit of the collar regularly. It is surprising how quickly a puppy grows and a collar can soon get very tight.

LEAD
Choose a lead to suit you, but make sure that the clip at the end is strong and secure and will not break.

An extending lead is ideal for relaxed walks, giving you security that your hound is under control but allowing him the chance to follow sniffs and enjoy himself. Again, there is a variety of different types on the market. The tape variety tends to get tangled up less than the cord ones. Remember, an extending lead should never be used when you are walking in busy, built-up areas. It only takes one lunge and your Beagle could be in the road – and this could have fatal consequences.

ID
It is important that your Beagle can be easily identified, in case he strays or gets lost. Most people microchip their dogs, and

There is a wide selection of toys that you can buy for your puppy.

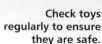

Check toys regularly to ensure they are safe.

breeders will often have puppies chipped before they leave for their new homes. Tattooing is another form of permanent ID; it is usually done inside the ear.

By law any dog in a public place must wear a collar with the name and address (including postcode) of the owner on it, or engraved on a tag, so you will need to get a tag cut for use when your puppy is ready to venture out. It is also good practice to state on the tag if your dog has been microchipped. Remember, it can be dangerous if a tag gets caught up or trapped in

a fence, when your puppy is unsupervised, so it is best not to use a tag in the home until he is older.

TOYS

This is where it is easy to get carried away in the pet shop. Buy two or three toys – perhaps a ball, a soft toy and a rope pull. You will have plenty of time to find out what he likes and buy them later on! Make sure that the toys you buy are robust enough to withstand chewing. A determined chewer will get the stuffing out of

soft toys, and will bite chunks out of plastic toys, which will cause major problems if swallowed.

GROOMING GEAR

Beagles take little grooming, so a brush and a couple of towels will suffice for a puppy. If you are going to clip your dog's nails, there are different designs on the market. Ask advice from your breeder or an experienced person so that you buy a pair that suits you. You will need shampoo once he gets a little older. Use specialist dog products and choose those containing as few chemicals as possible – ideally hypoallergenic – to minimise any irritation to sensitive skins. *For more information on grooming, see Chapter Five: The Best of Care.*

TRAVELLING BY CAR

You will need some form of restraint for your Beagle when he is travelling in the car so that he is under control at all times. It is safest to use a metal crate in the car, as detailed above, but if you cannot fit one in, look for safety harnesses or dog guards to make sure your dog is safe and secure and that you are within the law.

COLLECTING YOUR PUPPY

You have prepared your house and garden for the new arrival and bought the equipment you need, so now you are ready to collect your new puppy. In most cases, a breeder will be ready to release puppies at around eight weeks of age, though some may prefer to wait until they are 12 weeks old.

Hopefully you will have been to visit your puppy at least once and will have an idea of the journey and the time it takes. If it is a long journey, plan carefully so that you can make the journey as stress-free as possible for your puppy and yourself.

Before setting out, make a list of any questions you want to ask – it is so easy to forget in the excitement of collecting your new puppy – but don't be afraid of calling later if you have forgotten anything. Check on any training that has been started, such as house training.

Arrange to collect your puppy at a time that will suit both you and the breeder. Remember that the breeder may be sending several puppies off to their new homes on the same day, so try to keep to agreed times and let them know if you will be delayed (or early!).

By the time you collect your puppy, you should have made financial arrangements so that you are both happy with the agreed price and sale details. Check to see if your puppy's pedigree has any endorsements – such as breeding restrictions. Breeders have their own reasons for placing endorsements, which should be explained to you before, or at, the time of sale.

Once the sale is completed, you should be given the following:

- Your puppy's registration papers
- Three-generation pedigree (you may get an extended five-generation pedigree)
- Diet sheet
- Worming and vaccination programme
- Sale agreement and receipt
- Breed information
- Food starter pack
- Insurance information
- Vaccination and microchip documents (if any)
- A blanket with the scent of mother and home, and perhaps a familiar toy.

Hopefully the breeder will have organised feeding times so that your puppy has not just been fed (and therefore more likely to be sick), and has let the puppy out to play so that he will be tired and ready for a snooze on the way home. It doesn't always work out like this, but this is the ideal.

If possible, recruit a helper to look after your puppy in the car on the way home. Well-behaved

At last it is time to collect your puppy.

children are fine, but do not take the whole family, unless you have to, as it can add to the stress levels. The needs of the puppy should be considered first.

Take plenty of newspapers and spare blankets and towels in case your puppy is sick. If you are using a crate in the car, your puppy can travel in it (start as you mean to go on), but try to locate the crate next to a passenger so that the pup can be comforted if he gets distressed. A puppy will travel happily on a passenger's lap, but this should be on the back seat out of the way of the driver. Long journeys are not a problem for the puppy once he settles, but it is important to organise the timing to minimise the stress factor for all of you.

ARRIVING HOME

Hopefully your house will already be organised for the new puppy when you get home. He will need to go straight out into the garden to go to the toilet and, if he is a confident hound, he will enjoy a little wander around to orientate himself. In the house, make sure he knows where his water bowl and his bed are located. Once he has settled a little, give him a small meal from the breeder's food pack to help him feel at home. Give him plenty of time and space to get used to his new home, and make sure that excited children (and adults) do not chase after him or distress him by too much attention and noise.

Your puppy is moving to a strange, new world without the support of his mother and siblings, so if he is a little timid, reassure him and let him explore in his own time. He will soon get to know his new family and learn the new routines. Give him attention to socialise him, but also make sure he has plenty of time for sleep. At eight weeks, a puppy is still very much a baby and needs time to rest as well as play.

However tempting it might be, do not invite everyone in to see the new puppy as soon as he arrives or you will overpower him with too many people. He will be delighted to see them once he has settled in and feels confident in his new surroundings.

THE FIRST NIGHT

The first night can be lonely for a puppy used to sleeping with his brothers and sisters. If you plan that he will sleep in his crate or bed, put him to bed with his 'home' blanket and perhaps a toy or two and, hopefully, he will settle after a short period of protest. Some pups are more determined and can take a few nights to get used to being alone, but the best plan is to harden your heart and keep him where

Arriving in a new home is a daunting experience, even for the most confident puppy.

you want him to sleep. If he is really distressed, you could go down to reassure him that he has not been left, but do not make a fuss of him or his crying will be rewarded. Just check he is not in any trouble and then leave him. If you are using a crate, it might help to put a blanket over it so that he feels secure.

Some people recommend putting the crate in your bedroom for a couple of weeks until he has settled in, but I am not sure if this is a wise option, as the puppy will have to be alone at some stage. However, if he is truly distressed, it might be worth considering.

Establishing a routine is the key to successful house training.

HOUSE TRAINING

Remember that training starts as soon as your puppy arrives in his new home. Always take him out to relieve himself in the area you want him to use as a toileting area when he wakes up, immediately after a meal, and after a play session.

Stay with your pup until he has performed and praise him when he does. If you just put him outside and do not stay with him, he will try to follow you in again and will not concentrate on the job in hand. Be persistent and he should get the idea. When you leave him at night, place newspapers around his bed or in the crate. Take him out last thing before you put him to bed and first thing when you get him up.

During the day, try to keep an eye on your puppy to see signs of him wanting to relieve himself – he will usually start circling and

sniffing. If he starts to go in the house, pick him up and take him to the area of the garden that you wish him to use. If you cannot supervise him, put him in an area where he has access to outside and put newspapers down so that he will not get into the habit of going indoors.

If your puppy does mess or urinate in the house and you don't catch him in time, clear it up and spray the area with a pet stain/odour remover – available from most pet shops – to minimise the smell and, hopefully, discourage him from using the same spot again. It is no use disciplining your puppy if you do not catch him in the act, as he will not understand why you are annoyed with him. Just keep an eye on him so that you can establish good behaviour.

EARLY LEARNING

You should have decided on house rules before your youngster arrives home; the next stage is to train him to respect them. Be consistent. Beagles are intelligent hounds and soon work out if you really mean what you say. A puppy will soon pick out the ones in the family who will give in to him and let him have what he wants!

You must start with the intention of encouraging behaviour you want in an adult dog, so do not give in to him just because he is a cute little puppy. Remember that he is not a mind reader and needs to be told clearly what to do. Reinforce good behaviour with praise and/or rewards. Minimise the chance for bad behavior by not leaving things around and keeping doors and gates shut.

HANDLING

A puppy needs to be handled so that he accepts the attention without making a fuss.

Check the ears – they should be clean and odour-free.

Part the lips to check the teeth and gums.

However carefully you have planned and however well organised you are, your puppy will find things that he should not have, explore places that you thought he could not get into, and do things that you do not want him to do. At first, it is natural inquisitive behaviour and not 'naughty' in his terms. He is just doing what comes naturally. However, if he persists in behaviour you do not want, you must be assertive and show your displeasure.

HANDLING

Take time to give your puppy regular grooming sessions. At first it should be a gentle brush every few days or a rub down with a towel when he is wet after a walk. Make sure he gets used to accepting this as a normal part of his routine from when he is a small puppy. A puppy should not need bathing, but once he starts to go out and gets dirty (or smelly when he's rolled in something nasty) bathe him gently with warm water and dog shampoo, being careful not to make a fuss about it. Most Beagles are not keen on baths, so make sure he accepts them as part of his life and learns to tolerate them with good grace.

MEALTIMES

Beagles love their food, so *your* mealtimes can become a problem. Never feed a Beagle from the table or he will expect to be fed all the time and will be very demanding. Ideally, put him in his bed or a safe room away from the table with a chew or bone while you eat so that he does not associate your mealtimes with food for him.

STEALING

If your puppy 'steals' an item and runs off with it, do not chase after him or he will learn that stealing gets your attention and starts a wonderful game of chase. Instead, walk away, call him and offer a tasty treat in exchange for the thing he has stolen. This will teach him that bringing something back to you is a good way of getting your attention and a reward.

ESCAPING

At some stage your puppy may escape from the safety of the house or garden, so recall training is very important from an early age. Make a game of recall in the garden with plenty of rewards so that, when it counts and perhaps he does escape, he will want to come back to you.

Ideally, your fencing will be in good order, but if he finds a way out, mend it immediately. Otherwise, your Beagle will learn to actively find places to get out and will eventually become unmanageable.

Even if your fencing is secure, there are always those times when a neighbour calls and leaves the door open a little too long, or the postman leaves a gate open, and it is highly likely that your pup will go off to explore. If he escapes, do not chase after him or he will think you want to go exploring too! Contain your frustration, call him to you and offer a reward, making a big fuss of him when he comes so that next time he will want to come back to you. If you are angry with him when he comes back, he will not want to return another time, as he will be very wary of you.

CHEWING

It is natural for puppies to chew. They are teething for the first few months of their life, so provide toys, bones and chews to gnaw on. However, if you cannot supervise him, put him somewhere safe with the things he is allowed to chew so that you minimise the potential for him to do damage. Remember, it is not

There may be a time when your puppy attempts to stray from the safety of your garden.

his fault if people leave tempting items such as shoes or cuddly toys or perhaps the Christmas presents under the tree on the floor and he chews them. As far as he is concerned, they are put there for him and he will want to see what they taste like. It is up to the humans to get organised and keep things out of his way.

PLANNING ACTIVITIES

Beagles are intelligent hounds who love to be active and involved in doing things. If you do not find things for them to do, they will find activities for themselves, if only to get your attention. Be proactive: plan playtimes where you can both have fun and your puppy can learn new skills. This can include: retrieving a ball, hunting food or

toys hidden in the garden, hunting members of the family on walks, learning to do agility (but only when he is old enough), learning basic training, such as walking to heel, sit, and recall. With plenty of rewards for success, he will become a well-trained and happy young hound.

Finally, it is helpful if you are able to keep to a routine so that your Beagle knows what will be happening and what is expected of him. This helps training generally and toilet training in particular. If he is to be left during the day (certainly no more than up to four hours at a time), build this up slowly and get him used to being left so that he does not get distressed. He will understand that this is his routine and that you will be back with him soon.

For more information on training, see Chapter Six: Training and Socialisation.

VISITING THE VET

Contact your vet to arrange for a health check-up soon after your puppy arrives in his new home. This is usually a formality, but it is essential to confirm that your puppy is healthy and has no obvious problems. Breeders usually have their puppies veterinary checked before they leave for their new homes so that they are also certain that they are selling healthy puppies.

If your puppy has not had his

first vaccination or not been microchipped, this can be done during this first visit. The second vaccination is usually given at around 10 weeks, so book a date while you are there. You can also discuss worming and other health requirements. Most vets offer advice on neutering. This should only be done when the puppy is mature – bitches after their first season and dogs at around 9-12 months. Don't be persuaded to have the operation before this.

Make the visit to the vet enjoyable. If you are confident and happy, your puppy should be more relaxed about the visit. Offer a treat and praise him so he links visits to good experiences. Some vets give treats, which is always helpful. If you do not like the sight of needles, get someone else who is confident to take him in for his vaccination or microchipping.

Many vets offer annual health and worming programmes for an annual fee. It is cost effective to buy wormers on the internet or from a pet shop and follow the manufacturers' instructions if you are confident enough to do this, but if you are not, then it is worthwhile joining such a scheme. Vets will usually weigh your Beagle and give them health checks when you visit for the annual booster injection. These are worth taking up so that you can monitor his weight, check out for any possible health issues and keep him a slim, healthy Beagle. *For more information on health care, see Chapter Eight: Happy and Healthy.*

THE OUTSIDE WORLD

When your puppy has had his final vaccination and you have waited until he is safe to go out, the next stage is taking him out to socialise him and help him to be confident in the wider world.

WALKS

Start by taking your puppy for short, slow walks on the extending lead so that he can explore and become confident. Make sure he walks to heel, on a short lead when he is on pavements and needs to be under control in traffic, but where there is space and it is safe, let him have time on the extending lead to sniff and explore grass and hedges and meet other dogs and people.

Try to make sure that his early experiences are positive ones. Find other dog walkers who have friendly, obedient dogs whom he can play with and learn from. Watch out for dogs with temperament problems who might make him fearful of other dogs. Help him to mix with people in safe, relaxed situations so that he is friendly and outgoing. Most Beagles love human and canine company, but some are more timid or more dominant than others. This is the time when he will form his character – hopefully as a happy, confident well-adjusted hound.

IN THE CAR

If you are a car user, get your puppy used to going in the car as soon as possible. If he is travel sick, do not give up - take him on short journeys with a pleasant walk or visit to a friend at the end so that he associates it with pleasant activities. Gradually

In order to get the best from your Beagle you need to spend time with him, giving him mental stimulation.

extend the time he is in the car so that he overcomes his travel sickness.

TAKING ON A RESCUED DOG

If you are taking on an older, rescued Beagle, remember that he will probably take quite some time before he really settles in. Every Beagle behaves differently when they move to a new home. Some are angels for the first couple of weeks and then start to test the boundaries, while others will test you out immediately. Some are so distressed that they will cling to you and not want to let you out of their sight, while others decide this is 'home' and settle in very quickly.

Much of the planning will be exactly the same as for a puppy in terms of fencing, ground rules and house organisation. However, you will be taking on a Beagle that has lived with other people who probably had different priorities and ground rules – or possibly none at all! Firstly, try to get as much information as possible about the Beagle you are planning to take on. Why is he being rehomed? Has he been trained - and if so, how? Has he been used to going in a crate? Does he travel well in a car? Has he been used to being left at all? Using this information, you can plan how you will go about helping him to fit into your home and family. However, the information you have been given may not prove to be realistic, and often there is no information at all, so you will need to try out new situations

carefully and observe how your Beagle reacts.

Make sure you buy a secure collar with a tag with your details on it. If your Beagle is microchipped, transfer the ownership. Do make sure that your fences are in good condition and monitor your Beagle in the garden at first. Be very careful with open doors and gates. Some Beagles panic and try to find 'their' family, and others are superb escape artists (which is probably the reason for rehoming).

As with a puppy, set your ground rules – reward good behaviour and restrict the opportunity for bad behaviour. Do not leave your Beagle unattended until you are certain that he will not try to escape and will respect house rules. If you do have to leave him, put him in a safe room, where he can do little damage, or use a crate. If he has not been

used to a crate, get him used to it gradually, as some dogs will panic if they are put in confined spaces.

Take your Beagle's training slowly and carefully, and do not expect too much at once. Build up his trust, but equally be firm in establishing boundaries so that he knows that the humans are the ones that set the house rules.

SUMMARY

Taking on a new puppy or a rescued Beagle is very hard work if you aim to have a happy, well-balanced dog in the future. Taking shortcuts rarely works and you may end up with a very unhappy Beagle and even unhappier family. So plan carefully and think things through before your Beagle comes home with you. Take advice from your breeder and find as much specialist breed information as you can and you will be rewarded with a happy hound and family.

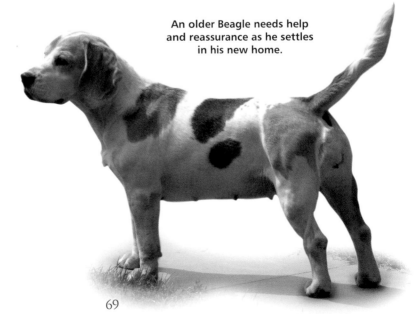

An older Beagle needs help and reassurance as he settles in his new home.

THE BEST OF CARE

Chapter 5

Beagles are relatively easy to care for, as they have no exaggerations in their structure and have short coats. However, to keep your companion in top condition you will need to understand some of the characteristics of the breed. Beagles are scent hounds, so usually put their heads down to catch exciting smells and will go for miles on walks.

They are very gregarious and love company, as they are not many generations removed from pack hounds. If there is only one dog in a family then, as far as he is concerned, the family is the pack. If you have just one Beagle, it is important to teach him to stay at home alone for a few hours so that you can keep appointments without your dog becoming stressed by being on his own. This can be done by leaving him for a very short time at first, making sure there are plenty of toys available. Gradually increase the time away and your Beagle will be content to be on his own for a couple of hours – and delighted to see you come home!

Most Beagles love their food, and sometimes anyone else's as well…

UNDERSTANDING NUTRITION

A balanced diet is as important for your Beagle as for yourself. You will need to ensure that the following components are provided in the correct quantities.

CARBOHYDRATES

These provide energy and some complex starchy carbohydrates help to maintain regular gut movements. Carbohydrates are broken down by the digestive system into sugars and starches; they are provided in the diet by biscuits, vegetables, rice and pulses.

FATS

Fats provide at least twice as much energy per gram as carbohydrates. The times when an extra energy source is required are when puppies are growing and for pregnant or lactating bitches. As with humans, unsaturated fats are healthier for your dog than saturated fats. Fatty acids are necessary for a healthy coat, good skin condition, the healing of wounds and an efficient reproductive system. Oily fish and vegetable sources are recommended.

PROTEIN

Protein is necessary for growth and the maintenance and repair of tissue. Protein includes a number of amino acids, some of which

Nutritional needs will change when there are increased demands, such as when a mother is feeding her puppies.

cannot be made by the body. Essential amino acids are contained in meat, fish, dairy products and eggs. Vegetables, cereals, and products such as Quorn contain many amino acids. However, you would need to be an expert in nutrition to maintain the correct balance, so if you wish to feed your Beagle a vegetarian diet it would probably be preferable to buy one of the many complete vegetarian foods available.

VITAMINS AND MINERALS
These are needed in small quantities. They are added to proprietary dog food and are found in most components of natural feeding. There needs to be a balance, so you should be careful not to overdo additives.

CHANGING NEEDS
A Beagle's needs will change as he develops from a puppy to an adult and then to old age. Puppies are fed four or five times a day when weaned, and to ensure correct growth and energy they need foods high in carbohydrates and fats. As they grow, their diet will change; protein content and the number of meals can be reduced. Some people feed an adult Beagle once a day, but many prefer to keep to two meals and this option is preferable for elderly Beagles.

Obviously, lifestyle influences the amount of food needed. A Beagle that is exercised for two hours a day will need more calories than one who only gets a short, daily walk. When your Beagle reaches his senior years he will probably not be taking so much exercise and his diet should be adjusted to reflect this. There are complete foods for senior dogs or you can continue the normal diet, adjusting the protein and possibly feeding two or three smaller meals each day. Never give bones from your Sunday roast to your puppy or adult Beagle, as these can splinter and cause injury to the intestines.

FEEDING METHODS

Most owners feed their Beagles at the same time each day – and it takes very little time for your Beagle to learn when the food should be in the dish. There is a school of thought that advocates 'free feeding': that is, allowing access to food at all times. I can only suppose the people who recommend this method have never owned a Beagle. Any Beagle in my house empties the dish of food within minutes, and if there are several in the home, the fast feeders would polish off the meal, leaving slower feeders with short rations.

Fasting is a feeding method that deprives the dog of food on one day per week. In theory, this gives the gut a rest and replicates feeding in the wild when there might not be food available. Complete foods are formulated to be fed every day, so if you choose a complete food you should not fast your dog once a week.

DIETARY CHOICES

If you are a new owner of any breed of dog, you may be surprised by the huge variety of dog food stocked by your local pet store. I will explain some of the choices, but it is important not to change the diet of your puppy too soon after he arrives in his new home or you will cause him to have an upset stomach. The breeder will have supplied you with a diet sheet, detailing the food that has been used, and

the timings of meals, since weaning.

Whichever type of food you choose, it is very important to teach your puppy good manners when it comes to mealtimes. As your puppy grows older, you can teach him to "Sit" and "Wait" before you put his bowl down, then use a simple word, maybe his name or "OK", to indicate he can have his food. This takes very little time to learn and it is a pleasure to see your happy Beagle sitting waiting for his food. If you have a number of Beagles and they all clamour and jump for their food, mealtimes can be very stressful for you unless you teach them all basic good manners.

It is also very important to teach your Beagle to accept you removing the feeding bowl if you

need to. The purpose of this is to teach your dog to accept your authority and to ensure he does not become possessive over food. If there are children near your dog at mealtimes, it is essential to prevent your dog being possessive over his food.

CHOOSING A DIET

If, as your puppy grows, you wish to change his diet, these are some of the options available:

COMPLETE DIETS

Complete foods are the most convenient way of ensuring your dog gets a balanced diet with all the vitamins and supplements he needs. Most manufacturers provide a range of foods from puppy to senior; these contain the right mix of protein,

A well-mannered Beagle will not worry if you approach him when he is eating.

A complete diet caters for all your dog's nutritional needs.

Most dogs find canned food very appetising.

You need a reliable supplier if you decide to feed fresh meat.

carbohydrate and minerals for each stage of your Beagle's development.

Guides to the correct amount are given on the pack. Do not be tempted to give more than the recommended amount or you will soon have a tubby Beagle. Some dogs develop allergies to certain foods. If this happens, your vet can test to see which foods should be avoided and will advise you on a suitable diet.

CANNED FOOD

Canned food and pouches are readily available in most pet shops or supermarkets. Good wholemeal biscuit should be fed with this. If shopping for your dog in a supermarket, do be careful not to buy a complete pellet food, thinking it is biscuit, because a complete food combined with tinned meat will lead to protein overload. A pet store is the best place to buy biscuit meal. It is important to soak this with boiling water and allow it to cool completely before mixing with meat. If dry meal is fed, it can lead to a condition called bloat; if this occurs, the dog's stomach will swell and it could be fatal. *For more information, see Chapter Eight: Happy and Healthy.*

HOMEMADE

If you choose to feed a diet of fresh meat and biscuit, you will need a reliable supplier of fresh or frozen meat and have the facilities to store it. My Beagle loves raw tripe and biscuit for her main meal. I buy the tripe frozen in blocks, which need to be completely thawed before feeding. One block lasts several days. A friend of mine, who has a number of Beagles, buys meat and offal from a butcher and cooks this before mixing with the meal. If you decide on this option, you will need to provide additional minerals and vitamins. Some Beagles love the addition of raw vegetables to their meal. A carrot or a broccoli stalk makes a healthy alternative to a chew stick.

BARF DIET

BARF stands for Biologically Appropriate Raw Food, or Bones And Raw Food, and is a holistic way of feeding. The diet reflects the way wild dogs would have eaten before they were domesticated. Raw meat, bones, skin and vegetables are included, but cereals, grains and preservatives are not. The mix of raw meat, vegetables and fruit should provide all the nourishment, vitamins and minerals dogs need. Other benefits of feeding the BARF include:
Teeth are kept clean naturally and gum disease is prevented.
The muscles of shoulder, jaw and neck are strengthened, as they are

used to rip at meaty bones. Stools are smaller and firmer. It is an economical diet.

The diet is based on feeding a balance of raw meat, fruit and vegetables, liquidised to make them more digestible. The ratio of meat to vegetables is 1:2. Raw bones should be fed once to twice a week and raw offal once a week. A variety of meats, fruit and vegetables will ensure your dog gets all the nutrients he needs.

If you decide to change to this diet, do it gradually over a two-week period. There are lots of books and helpful information available on the internet if you think this is the right choice for your Beagle.

FADDY FEEDERS

Beagles usually enjoy their food and it is best to stay with the regime you have selected once your Beagle is an adult. Unless there is a veterinary reason to change the diet, keep to your chosen method. A little variety can be a good thing, but beware of constantly offering different tastes, as this could lead to your pet becoming a faddy feeder and refusing on Wednesday what he enjoyed on Sunday. Beagles are thinking hounds and will soon learn that to refuse a straightforward meal may lead to the addition of tasty toppings.

Avoid scraps from the table; they may not be appropriate food for your dog and a Beagle pestering you when you are enjoying a meal is a sure way to shorten your temper.

Do not allow your Beagle to become picky, or he will always be waiting for some tasty additions.

PROTEIN OVERLOAD

Protein overload can lead to your Beagle becoming over-excitable and unruly. If you notice your usually placid companion developing these traits, it may be worth checking his food. Puppies kept on complete puppy foods into adult life are getting more calories than they need so have more energy to burn.

BEAGLE FATTIES

Beagles kept as pets can become overweight. They are very good at letting their owners know they are 'starving' despite having just had their rations. You may think that just one more biscuit cannot do any harm, but it can. If you cannot feel your Beagle's ribs or see a waist when you look down on him from above, he is carrying too much weight. This leads to a variety of health problems. An overweight Beagle may have difficulty walking for more than a short distance and have trouble with slopes and steps. It really is not kind to let your Beagle eat too much, as a Beagle fatty will not live as long as a slim one.

While walking recently, I met people with a Beagle I thought was at least eight years old; I was very surprised to learn she was just two. An overweight Beagle is lethargic and his quality of life will suffer.

A lean, fit Beagle will have a better quality of life and an increased life expectancy.

It can be a challenge to control your Beagle's weight. Some years ago, visitors often asked why the chairs at either end of the small kitchen table were connected by a rubber bungee usually used on car-roof racks. The answer was that it stopped Jolly, my Beagle, from pushing one of the chairs up to the work-top and using it as a step to gain access to anything tasty, even a loaf of bread that was sitting on top. Another of Jolly's talents was to open the fridge with a flick of a foot. Childproof door locks were tried, but he could deal with these. The solution was a small metal bolt drilled to the side of the fridge. If anyone tells me that Beagles are stupid, I give them these examples to prove that they are more than capable of solving problems.

If you are worried about your Beagle's weight, consult your veterinary surgeon, who will help you work out a diet for your dog.

TREATING YOUR BEAGLE

If you visit a pet food store, you will see many different treats for dogs. Some small, dry shapes can be used as training aids and as rewards for a good dog when he comes when called or whistled. However, do not forget to subtract the amount from your Beagle's daily allowance or your companion may lose his slim outline.

If you buy bones, either raw or roasted, you should teach your Beagle to give up the bone when you ask him to. This will prevent him becoming possessive over food or treats. This is particularly important if you have children.

Some types of treats can be dangerous if your Beagle is not supervised while chewing them. Rawhide chews seem to be universally available as a treat, but small pieces can be swallowed and stay undigested in the gut. This can lead to a blockage, which, in the worst case, will require an operation. Some of the small, compressed, composite chews are highly coloured and can affect the colour of excreta.

Dental chews are useful for cleaning the teeth and keeping gums healthy. Another good option is a sterilised white bone, with or without a tasty filling. My two-year-old Beagle gnaws on hers every evening for about 30 minutes.

USING ADDITIVES

If your choice for food is a complete diet, you should not need to supplement it. The meat and biscuit option can be supplemented by cod liver or evening primrose oil to improve the coat. Other oils, such as sunflower or olive oil, can help older dogs that have stiff joints. Some people believe the use of garlic, in tablet form, repels fleas and while there is no proven research to support this theory, it can be effective. In pale-coloured Beagles, supplementing seaweed powder can improve the pigmentation of the nose.

Bones and chews should be given under supervision.

GROOMING BEAGLES

Beagle coats are easily kept clean with a quick brush every day. Beagles enjoy this time and usually come quickly when the grooming tools appear. You can start by using a bristle brush, which helps to distribute the natural oils in the coat. Then use a hound glove, which has very fine pins on one side and a buffing material on the other, to produce a shine. When your Beagle sheds his coat, a fine comb or a rubber tool with large, round pins will remove unwanted hair.

A thorough rub with a dog towel is probably all that is needed after a walk in wet weather. However, if your Beagle's legs and feet are caked in mud after cross-country exercise, putting one foot at a time in a basin of tepid water will pay off. Beagles follow scents and are particularly fond of anything smelly. If your dog finds something 'choice', he is likely to roll in it. Fox excreta is a favourite (as is skunk in the USA) and both have the most awful smell. A friend recently told me that following a bath, tomato ketchup rubbed into the coat will remove the residual smell of fox, and apparently it eliminates the smell of skunk as well. I would hasten to add that you will need to rinse the ketchup out!

You can bath your Beagle whenever necessary. Clean bedding helps to keep him free from odour, and regular changes of bedding are also a good

COAT CARE

Grooming with a bristle brush helps to distribute the natural oils in the coat.

A rake helps to remove dead hair when your Beagle is shedding.

There are times when your Beagle has rolled – and a bath is essential!

preventative measure to take against fleas. If you spot a flea while grooming, there are suitable sprays and shampoos. Some 'spot-on' treatments can cause irritation in paler hounds, so I use tablets. You should not treat a young puppy for fleas without getting advice from your vet.

Grooming also gives the opportunity to monitor changes in your dog's skin or coat, and you can consult your vet if there is any cause for concern.

EARS
A Beagle's ears are relatively long and hang down close to the face. As a result, air does not circulate inside them and they can become dirty. Check ears on a weekly basis and, if necessary, clean them with a proprietary ear cleaner. If there is a discharge that smells, consult your vet.

TEETH
Teeth should be inspected regularly. Chewing bones, raw

ROUTINE CARE

Clean the ears with cotton-wool (cotton) – but do not probe too deeply.

Wipe the eyes to get rid of debris.

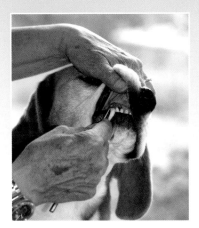

Teeth can be brushed or scaled to prevent the build-up of tartar.

Nails will need to be trimmed on a routine basis.

marrowbones, and the chews previously mentioned helps to remove tartar and keep the gums healthy. If the teeth appear dirty, you can clean them with a dog toothbrush and specially formulated toothpaste; human toothpaste should not be used. If there is a build-up of tartar, your vet may advise you to have the teeth cleaned under anaesthetic.

NAILS
If you give your Beagle long walks on hard surfaces, his nails should stay short. However, if his main exercise is on grass, you will need to keep a check on their length, as they grow quickly and will need to be clipped or filed. When clipping, it is only the tip that should be cut or the quick may bleed. If you are not confident, ask a nurse at your veterinary surgery to do it. Do pay attention to nails; a Beagle with long nails that are beginning to curl is a sorry sight and he will not be able to enjoy walks.

SHOW PRESENTATION

If you are intending to show your Beagle, you do not need to spend hours on preparation; the regular attention you give to teeth, nails and coat will suffice. Bear in mind that a clean hound will be appreciated by the judge at a Championship show, as they will probably have over 100 Beagles to examine. Even at the smaller shows, dirty hounds cannot expect top honours.

Some Beagles have especially thick coats where the base of the neck joins the back. This makes the neck look stuffy instead of the elegant outline that is desired. Specialist rakes are available for use here. It is a good idea to ask an experienced friend to show you how to use them effectively, as it is possible to irritate the skin by over-enthusiastic use.

Sometimes in Europe and America, exhibitors over-trim Beagles' tails. This is beginning to be seen in the British show ring. The Breed Standard, the written blueprint for the breed in Europe, states that the tail should be: "well covered with hair, especially on the underside". The Standard published by the American Kennel Club ends the description of the tail: "with brush" and in the defects states: "Rat tail with absence of brush". So both the European and American Standards require a tail with a

The Beagle must look immaculate for the judge's inspection.

good covering of hair.

Cutting the hair off square at the end of the tail, and stripping out the underside, leaves the Beagle with a thin, whippy tail, which is not at all typical of the breed.

If you use conditioner on your Beagle's coat, you should be aware of regulations prohibiting preparations being left in the coat at shows.

EXERCISE

Beagle puppies should not have a great amount of exercise in their first year, as their bones are growing and their joints need to develop. Puppies run around and play, and then fall asleep when nature tells them they have done enough. Formal exercise should be kept to a minimum. A guide to the correct amount is

approximately one minute of exercise for every week of his age – for example, a 15-week-old puppy requires 15 minutes. Too much exercise, or allowing a puppy to jump down steps on to a hard surface, can lead to injury or bones not developing properly.

You can increase the exercise as your Beagle reaches adulthood. Beagles, being descended from hunting hounds, enjoy galloping with their noses down to catch a scent. Unless you are lucky enough to have a space for free running, which is secure and free from traffic, you may have to restrict your walks to exercise on the lead. For roadwork on the lead, an hour a day is usually the minimum.

Your Beagle will adapt to the exercise you can offer. I used to take my Beagles on a bridle path between arable fields. They loved to run, noses down, and would sometimes put up rabbit or hare – although they never caught them! Before I let them off the lead, I would blow three short blasts on a gundog whistle and give them each a small biscuit. When they were off the lead and on the far side of the field, three blasts on the whistle would soon have them back with me, looking for their treats.

If you walk in a rural area, you need to be aware of livestock, and keep him on a lead if there are

EXERCISE

A puppy will get as much exercise as he needs playing in the garden.

Provide opportunities for your Beagle to use his nose.

A game of retrieve is an excellent form of exercise.

any animals nearby. There are restrictions at certain times of the year regarding exercising dogs on beaches, and it is your responsibility to respect these regulations.

Finally, and most importantly, make sure you clear up any mess left by your dog and dispose of it correctly.

Not all Beagles will chase and retrieve a ball or a toy, but if you can interest yours in doing so, it will add another activity to his daily routine.

BEAGLE OLDIES

Beagles are a healthy breed and usually live between 10 and 15 years. I had an old lady, named Hopeful, who reached the grand old age of 17. The older Beagle has very different needs from a puppy, and, as with people, adjustments need to be made to their lifestyle.

An older Beagle will not need as many calories as a youngster, but do not make sudden changes to the diet or his digestive system may suffer. There are specialist senior diets available, and if you are feeding a complete diet, it will be a simple matter to make the change gradually. It may also be helpful to your pet if you feed twice a day instead of once. If you do, remember to divide the daily ration in half. It is also important to check an elderly Beagle's teeth for the build-up of tartar.

A Beagle's needs will change as he grows older.

Older Beagles still love exercise, but they will not have the stamina to walk for miles and will generally be slower. Your dog may develop arthritis, in which case your vet will advise on treatment. If you have several dogs, you may need to adapt your regular exercise programme to give the young ones the time they need without putting undue strain on your oldie. My 17-year-old Beagle, Hopeful, loved the idea of a walk and was delighted when the lead was produced. However, a stroll to the end of the drive was enough and she turned back of her own accord, satisfied that she had had her daily airing.

Bladder control may be less reliable and you should be aware of this and let your dog out more frequently.

Warmth and freedom from draughts are very important for an elderly Beagle, so if he has been sleeping happily on a fleecy mat, you might consider a moulded plastic bed with fleece inside. The high back will give added protection.

Your Beagle's coat will probably become harsher and grooming should be regular but gentle. Nails should still be given attention, as they will not be worn down with shorter walks. It is possible that sight and hearing will deteriorate, so you might not get the response you expect when you call your dog – but his ability to find a scent will usually remain sharp.

Remember, these changes will come gradually and your companion is the same one he was 10 years before: he wants to enjoy life and play the same games, just not for such long periods or so vigorously. If you have children, an elderly dog will teach them to adapt and be tolerant. The most important lesson my family learnt from dear Hopeful was patience!

SAYING GOODBYE

The time will come when your faithful friend's health fails and you will have to decide whether to treat the condition or opt for euthanasia. Before deciding which path to follow, you should consider the following factors:

In time, you will be able to look back and remember all the happy times you spent with your beloved Beagle.

- Is your Beagle still enjoying a good quality of life?
- If your dog is on medication, are there side-effects that cause discomfort?
- Are you delaying a decision because you cannot bear the finality of what might be the right thing to do?

You will know how much your dog can enjoy life. My Hopeful followed the routine of the walk down the drive for almost a year, then one morning she did not want to get out of bed. So we knew it was time.

It is never easy, but if you do not face up to reality, you are doing your friend a disservice. If there is an option of surgery, your vet should be able to help you evaluate the impact on your dog and whether there will be ongoing drug treatment that may have severe side-effects. Keeping a dog alive because you want him to be there for you is a selfish choice. Your Beagle has been your friend for many years, and a peaceful and stress-free end to his life is the last gift you can give him. Talk to your vet and seek his expert advice.

When the time comes, try to make everything as easy as you can for your dog. Some dogs find a visit to the surgery stressful; if this is the case, a home visit can be arranged and this will be a much calmer occasion.

Many vets now arrange for cremation as an alternative to burial. You can have the ashes returned to you and bury or scatter them where you choose. If you select part of your garden for this, it will always be a special place where you can remember your friend.

The grief following the loss of a much-loved Beagle can affect owners profoundly. Sometimes people outside your family cannot understand that your dog was such an important part of your life and are therefore not as sympathetic as you might wish. If your lost friend was the only Beagle in your house, some will suggest a replacement. They do not understand that a new Beagle will not be a replacement. When you are ready for another dog, he will have his own personality and will take his place in your family, complementing the memory of your previous friend.

If you suffer too deeply from loss, there are pet bereavement counsellors who may be able to help. The internet is another resource where there are befriending groups for people in the same situation.

If you have other dogs, they will be affected by the loss of their companion and may need some extra attention.

In these difficult days, remember all the good times you shared and be comforted by the knowledge that you took the decision to save your beloved Beagle from suffering.

SOCIALISATION AND TRAINING

Chapter 6

When you decided to bring a Beagle into your life, you probably had dreams of how it was going to be: long walks together, cosy evenings with a Beagle lying devotedly at your feet and whenever you returned home, there would always be a special welcome waiting for you.

There is no doubt that you can achieve all this – and much more – with a Beagle, but like anything that is worth having, you must be prepared to put in the work. A Beagle, regardless of whether he is a puppy or an adult, does not come ready trained, understanding exactly what you want and fitting perfectly into your lifestyle. A Beagle has to learn his place in your family and he must discover what is acceptable behaviour.

We have a great starting point in that the breed has a sound, out-going temperament. The Beagle was developed to hunt using outstanding scenting ability, and although he retains a strong work ethic, he is friendly and sociable and is happy to co-operate with his human family. He is also highly intelligent, with a stubborn, determined streak, so you must be on your mettle in order to bring out the best in him.

THE FAMILY PACK

Dogs have been domesticated for some 14,000 years, but luckily for us, they have inherited and retained behaviour from their distant ancestor – the wolf. A Beagle may never have lived in the wild, but he is born with the survival skills and the mentality of a meat-eating predator who hunts in a pack. A wolf living in a pack owes its existence to mutual co-operation and an acceptance of a hierarchy, as this ensures both food and protection. A domesticated dog living in a family pack has exactly the same outlook. He wants food, companionship, and leadership – and it is your job to provide for these needs.

YOUR ROLE

Theories about dog behaviour and methods of training go in and out of fashion, but, in reality, nothing has changed from the day when wolves ventured in from the wild to join the family circle. The wolf (and equally the dog) accepts a subservient place in the family pack in return for food and protection. In a dog's eyes, you are his leader and he relies on you to make all the important decisions. This does not mean that you have to act like a dictator or a bully. You are accepted as a

**Are you ready
to take on the
role as leader?**

leader, without argument, as long as you have the right credentials.

The first part of the job is easy. You are the provider and you are therefore respected because you supply food. In a Beagle's eyes, you must be the ultimate hunter, because a day never goes by when you cannot find food. The second part of the leader's job description is straightforward, but for some reason we find it hard to achieve. In order for a dog to accept his place in the family pack, he must respect his leader as the decision-maker. A low-ranking pack animal does not question authority; he is perfectly happy to see someone else shoulder the responsibility. Problems will only arise if you cut a poor figure as leader and the dog feels he should mount a challenge for the top-ranking role.

HOW TO BE A GOOD LEADER

There are a number of guidelines to follow to establish yourself in the role of leader in a way that your Beagle understands and respects. If you have a puppy, you may think you don't have to take this on board for a few months, but that would be a big mistake. With a Beagle it is absolutely essential to start as you mean to go on. This is a breed that is clever enough to work things out and will decide whether to co-operate or not. The behaviour he learns as a puppy will continue throughout his adult life, which means that undesirable behaviour can be difficult to rectify.

When your Beagle first arrives in his new home, follow these guidelines:

- **Keep it simple:** Decide on the rules you want your Beagle to obey and always make it 100 per cent clear what is acceptable – and what is unacceptable – behaviour.
- **Be consistent:** If you are not consistent about enforcing rules, how can you expect your Beagle to take you seriously? There is nothing worse than allowing your Beagle to jump on the sofa one moment and then scolding him the next time he does it because he is muddy. As far as the Beagle is concerned, he may as well try it on because he can't predict your reaction. Bear in mind, inconsistency leads to insecurity.
- **Get your timing right:** If you are rewarding your Beagle and

86

THE THINKING BEAGLE
This is a breed that works things out – to his own advantage.

This kong is out of reach but something can be done…

Standing on his hindlegs, the Beagle sizes up the problem.

By stretching up and reaching with his paws, he rolls the kong towards him.

One more push…

Got it!

You need to tune into your Beagle's body language. These dogs may look menacing but it is all one big game.

equally if you are reprimanding him, you must respond within one to two seconds otherwise the dog will not link his behaviour with your reaction (see page 93).

- **Read your dog's body language:** Find out how to read body language and facial expressions (see page 91) so that you understand your Beagle's feelings and intentions.
- **Be aware of your own body language:** You can help your dog to learn by using your body language to communicate with him. For example, if you want your dog to come to you, open your arms out and look inviting. If you want your dog to stay, use a hand signal (palm flat, facing the dog) so you are effectively 'blocking' his advance.
- **Tone of voice:** Dogs do not speak English; they learn by associating a word with the

required action. However, they are very receptive to tone of voice, so you can use your voice to praise him or to correct undesirable behaviour. If you are pleased with your Beagle, praise him to the skies in a warm, happy voice. If you want to stop him raiding the bin, use a deep, stern voice when you say "No".

- **Give one command only:** If you keep repeating a command, or keep changing it, your Beagle will think you are babbling and will probably ignore you. If your Beagle does not respond the first time you ask, make it simple by using a treat to lure him into position and then you can reward him for a correct response.
- **Daily reminders:** A young, ebullient Beagle is apt to forget his manners from time to time and an adolescent dog may

attempt to challenge your authority (see page 105). Rather than coming down on your Beagle like a ton of bricks when he does something wrong, try to prevent bad manners by daily reminders of good manners. For example:

i Do not let your dog barge ahead of you when you are going through a door.

ii Do not let him leap out of the car the moment you open the door (which could be potentially lethal, as well as being disrespectful).

iii Do not let him eat from your hand when you are at the table.

iv Do not let him 'win' a toy at the end of a play session and then make off with it. You 'own' his toys and you 'allow' him to play with them. Your Beagle must learn to give up a toy when you ask.

UNDERSTANDING YOUR BEAGLE

Body language is an important means of communication between dogs, which they use to make friends, to assert status and to avoid conflict. It is important to get on your dog's wavelength by understanding his body language and reading his facial expressions.

- A positive body posture and a wagging tail indicate a happy, confident dog.
- A crouched body posture with ears back and tail down show that a dog is being submissive. A dog may do this when he is being told off or if a more assertive dog approaches him.
- A bold dog will stand tall, looking strong and alert. His ears will be forward and his tail will be held high.
- A dog who raises his hackles (lifting the fur along his topline) is trying to look as scary as possible.
- A playful dog will go down on his front legs while standing on his hind legs in a bow position. This friendly invitation says: "I'm no threat, let's play." Beagles are very friendly, playful dogs, and you will see this behaviour when they are interacting with other dogs, and when they are trying to initiate a game with their human playmates.
- A dominant, aggressive dog will meet other dogs with a hard stare. If he is challenged, he may bare his teeth and growl and the corners of his mouth will be drawn forward. His ears will be forward and he will appear tense in every muscle.
- A nervous dog will often show aggressive behaviour as a means of self-protection. If threatened, this dog will lower his head and flatten his ears. The corners of his mouth may be drawn back and he may bark or whine.
- Some Beagles are 'smilers', curling up their top lip and showing their teeth when they greet people. This should never be confused with a snarl, which would be accompanied by the upright posture of a dominant dog. A smiling dog will have a low body posture and a wagging tail; he is being submissive and it is a greeting that is often used when low-ranking animals greet high-ranking animals in a pack.
- Beagles tend to run in circles when playing and chasing. This goes back to their hunting roots, as their quarry, the hare, always runs a circle.

GIVING REWARDS

Why should your Beagle do as you ask? If you follow the guidelines given above, your Beagle should respect your authority, but what about the time when he is playing with a

For most Beagles, a food reward provides a good incentive to work.

Some Beagles prefer to be rewarded with a toy.

new doggy friend or has found a really enticing scent? The answer is that you must always be the most interesting, the most attractive and the most irresistible person in your Beagle's eyes. It would be nice to think that you could achieve this by personality alone, but most of us need a little extra help. You need to find out what is the biggest reward for your dog. In virtually every case, a Beagle will be motivated to work for a food reward. Some enjoy a game with a toy – particularly a squeaky toy – but generally food works best for training. Whatever reward you use, make sure it is something that your dog really wants.

When you are teaching a dog a new exercise, you should reward your Beagle frequently. When he knows the exercise or command,

reward him randomly so that he keeps on responding to you in a positive manner.

If your Beagle does something extra special, like leaving a scent and coming back to you, make sure he knows how pleased you are by giving him a handful of treats or throwing his toy a few extra times. If he gets a bonanza reward, he is more likely to come back on future occasions because you have proved to be even more rewarding than his previous activity.

TOP TREATS

Some trainers grade treats depending on what they are asking the dog to do. A dog may get a low-grade treat (such as a piece of dry food) to reward good behaviour on a random basis, such as sitting when you open a

door or allowing you to examine his teeth. High-grade treats (which may be cooked liver, sausage or cheese) may be reserved for training new exercises, or for use in the park when you want a really good recall, for example.

Whatever type of treat you use, you should remember to subtract it from your Beagle's daily food ration. Beagles love their food and it does not take many extra treats for them to pile on the pounds. Fat dogs are lethargic, prone to health problems and will almost certainly have a shorter life expectancy, so reward your Beagle but always keep a check on his figure!

HOW DO DOGS LEARN?

It is not difficult to get inside your Beagle's head and understand how he learns, as it is not dissimilar to the way we learn. Dogs learn by conditioning: they find out that specific behaviours produce specific consequences. This is known as operant conditioning or consequence learning. Consequences have to be immediate or clearly linked to the behaviour, as a dog sees the world in terms of action and result. Dogs will quickly learn if an action has a bad consequence or a good consequence.

Dogs also learn by association. This is known as classical conditioning or association learning. It is the type of learning made famous by Pavlov's experiment with dogs. Pavlov presented dogs with food and measured their salivary response

THE CLICKER REVOLUTION

Karen Pryor pioneered the technique of clicker training when she was working with dolphins. It is very much a continuation of Pavlov's work and makes full use of association learning. Karen wanted to mark 'correct' behaviour at the precise moment it happened. She found it was impossible to toss a fish to a dolphin when it was in mid-air, when she wanted to reward it. Her aim was to establish a conditioned response so the dolphin knew that it had performed correctly and a reward would follow.

The solution was the clicker: a small matchbox-shaped training aid, with a metal tongue that makes a click when it is pressed. To begin with, the dolphin had to learn that a click meant that food was coming. The dolphin then learnt that it must 'earn' a click in order to get a reward. Clicker training has been used with many different animals, most particularly with dogs, and it has proved hugely successful. It is a great aid for pet owners and is also widely used by professional trainers who are training highly specialised skills.

(how much they drooled). Then he rang a bell just before presenting the food. At first, the dogs did not salivate until the food was presented. But after a while they learnt that the sound of the bell meant that food was coming and so they salivated when they heard the bell. A dog needs to learn the association in order for it to have any meaning. For example, a dog that has never seen a lead before will be completely indifferent to it. A dog that has learnt that a lead means he is going for a walk will get excited the second he sees the lead; he has learnt to associate a lead with a walk.

BE POSITIVE

The most effective method of training dogs is to use their ability to learn by consequence and to teach that the behaviour you want produces a good consequence. For example, if you ask your Beagle to "Sit" and reward him with a treat, he will learn that it is worth his while to sit on command because it will lead to a treat. He is far more likely to repeat the behaviour, and the behaviour will become stronger, because it results in a positive outcome. This method of training is known as positive reinforcement and it generally leads to a happy, co-operative dog that is willing to work and a handler who has fun training his dog.

The opposite approach is negative reinforcement. This is far less effective and often results in a poor relationship between dog and owner. In this method of training, you ask your Beagle to "Sit" and if he does not respond, you deliver a sharp yank on the training collar or push his rear to the ground. The dog learns that not responding to your command has a bad consequence and he may be less likely to ignore you in the future. However, it may well have a bad consequence for you, too. A dog that is treated in this way may associate harsh handling with the handler and become aggressive or fearful. Instead of establishing a pattern of willing co-operation, you are establishing a relationship built on coercion. The Beagle is particularly sensitive to harsh handling, and if he experiences this treatment he will not work with you but against you.

GETTING STARTED

As you train your Beagle you will develop your own techniques as you get to know what motivates him. You may decide to get involved with clicker training or you may prefer to go for a simple command-and-reward formula. It does not matter what form of training you use, as long as it is based on positive, reward-based methods.

There are a few important guidelines to bear in mind when you are training your Beagle:

- Find a training area that is free from distractions, particularly when you are just starting out. The Beagle loves to use his nose, so it may be easier to train him indoors to begin with.
- Keep training sessions short, especially with young puppies that have short attention spans.

- Do not train if you are in a bad mood or if you are on a tight schedule – the training session will be doomed to failure.
- If you are using a toy as a reward, make sure it is only available when you are training. In this way it has an added value for your Beagle.
- If you are using food treats, make sure they are bite-size and easy to swallow; you don't want to hang about while your Beagle chews on his treat.
- Do not attempt to train your Beagle after he has eaten, or soon after returning from exercise. He will either be too full up to care about food treats or too tired to concentrate.
- When you are training, move around your allocated area so that your dog does not think that an exercise can only be

The Beagle is easily distracted by scents, so you may find training indoors easier to start with.

performed in one place.

- If your Beagle is finding an exercise difficult, try not to get frustrated. Go back a step and praise him for his effort. You will probably find he is more successful when you try again at the next training session.
- If a training session is not going well – either because you are in the wrong frame of mind or the dog is not focusing – ask your Beagle to do something you know he can do (such as a trick he enjoys performing) and then you can reward him with a food treat or a play with his favourite toy, ending the session on a happy, positive note.
- Do not train for too long. You need to end a training session on a high, with your Beagle wanting more, rather than making him sour by asking too much from him.

In the exercises that follow, clicker training is introduced and followed, but all the exercises will work without the use of a clicker.

INTRODUCING A CLICKER

This is easy, and the intelligent Beagle will learn about the clicker in record time! It can be combined with attention training, which is a very useful tool and

You can teach the "Watch" command at the same time as you introduce the clicker.

can be used on many different occasions.

- Prepare some treats and go to an area that is free from distractions. Allow your Beagle to wander and when he stops to look at you, click and reward by throwing him a treat. This means he will not crowd you, but will go looking for the treat. Repeat a couple of times. If your Beagle is very easily distracted, you may need to start this exercise with the dog on a lead.
- After a few clicks, your Beagle will understand that if he hears a click, he will get a treat. He must now learn that he must 'earn' a click. This time, when your Beagle looks at you, wait a

little longer before clicking and then reward him. If your Beagle is on a lead but responding well, try him off the lead.

- When your Beagle is working for a click and giving you his attention, you can introduce a cue or command word, such as "Watch". Repeat a few times, using the cue. You now have a Beagle that understands the clicker and will give you his attention when you ask him to "Watch".

TRAINING EXERCISES

A Beagle enjoys being busy and occupied, and so training sessions should be fun and enjoyed by both of you. There is no doubting the Beagle's intelligence, but he can be stubborn, making it difficult to change his mindset. Be creative with your training to make it varied and interesting; if you hit a problem, do not be confrontational but invent a new way of training an exercise. Watch out for the Beagle's legendary ability to feign; he will pretend he is trying to do as you ask, but he is really working out if it is worth his while. Hard though it may be, never laugh at a Beagle's antics to his face, or he will sense he has the upper hand and that will be the end of co-operation.

To start with, lure your Beagle into the Sit.

Lower a treat to the ground, and your Beagle will follow it, going into the Down position.

THE SIT

This is the easiest exercise to teach, so it is rewarding for both you and your Beagle.

- Choose a tasty treat and hold it just above your puppy's nose. As he looks up at the treat, he will naturally go into the 'Sit'. As soon as he is in position, reward him.
- Repeat the exercise and when your pup understands what you want, introduce the "Sit" command.
- You can practise the Sit exercise at mealtimes by holding out the bowl and waiting for your dog to sit. Most Beagles learn this one very quickly!

THE DOWN

Work hard at this exercise because a reliable 'Down' is useful in many different situations, and an instant 'Down' can be a lifesaver.

- You can start with your dog in a 'Sit', or it is just as effective to teach it when the dog is standing. Hold a treat just below your puppy's nose and slowly lower it towards the ground. The treat acts as a lure and your puppy will follow it, first going down on his forequarters and then bringing his hindquarters down as he tries to get the treat.

- Make sure you close your fist around the treat and only reward your puppy with the treat when he is in the correct position. If your puppy is reluctant to go 'Down', you can apply gentle pressure on his shoulders to encourage him to go into the correct position.
- When your puppy is following the treat and going into position, introduce a verbal command.
- Build up this exercise over a period of time, each time waiting a little longer before giving the reward, so the puppy learns to stay in the 'Down' position.

THE RECALL

It is never too soon to begin teaching your Beagle the recall. Remember, the Beagle is a hound with a strong instinct to follow a scent, so off-lead exercise provides an endless source of stimulation, and selective deafness may well take over… You must allow your Beagle to use his nose and behave like a dog, but you must teach him when it is time to return to your side.

Hopefully, the breeder will have already started recall training by calling the puppies in from outside and rewarding them with some treats scattered on the floor. But even if this has not been the case, you will find that a puppy arriving in his new home is highly responsive. His chief desire is to follow you and be with you. Capitalise on this from day one by getting your pup's attention and calling him to you in a bright, excited tone of voice.

You want to build up a happy, positive response to the Recall.

- Practise in the garden. When your puppy is busy exploring, get his attention by calling his name and, as he runs towards you, introduce the verbal command "Come". Make sure you sound happy and exciting, so your puppy wants to come to you. When he responds, give him lots of praise.

- If your puppy is slow to respond, try running away a few paces, or jumping up and down. It doesn't matter how silly you look, the key issue is to get your puppy's attention and then make yourself irresistible!

- In a dog's mind, coming when called should be regarded as the best fun because he knows he is always going to be rewarded. Never make the mistake of telling your dog off, no matter how slow he is to respond, as you will undo all your previous hard work.

- When you call your Beagle to you, make sure he comes up close enough to be touched. He must understand that "Come" means that he should come right up to you, otherwise he will think that he can approach and then veer off when it suits him.

- When you are free running your dog, make sure you have his favourite toy or a pocket full of treats so you can reward him at intervals throughout the walk as you call him to you. Do not allow your dog to free run and only call him back at the end of the walk to clip on his lead. An intelligent Beagle will soon realise that the recall means the end of his walk and then end of fun – so who can blame him for not wanting to come back?

SECRET WEAPON

You can build up a strong recall by using another form of association learning. Buy a whistle and when you are giving your Beagle his food, peep on the whistle. You can choose the type of signal you want to give: two short peeps or one long whistle, for example. Within a matter of days, your dog will learn that the sound of the whistle means that food is coming.

Now transfer the lesson outside. Arm yourself with some tasty treats and the whistle. Allow your Beagle to run free in the garden and after a couple of minutes, use the whistle. The dog has already learnt to associate the whistle with food, so he will come towards you. Immediately reward him with a treat and lots of praise. Repeat the lesson a few times in the garden, so you are confident that your dog is

responding before trying it in the park. Make sure you always have some treats in your pocket when you go for a walk and your dog will quickly learn how rewarding it is to come to you.

Whistle training seems to work particularly well with Beagles, as the shrill sound seems to penetrate their consciousness – even when they are following the most tantalising scent!

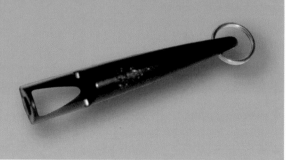

TRAINING LINE

This is the equivalent of a very long lead, which you can buy at a pet store, or you can make your own with a length of rope. The training line is attached to your Beagle's collar and should be around 15 feet (4.5 metres) in length.

The purpose of the training line is to prevent your Beagle from disobeying you so that he never has the chance to get into bad habits. For example, when you call your Beagle and he ignores you, you can immediately pick up

the end of the training line and call him again. By picking up the line you will have attracted his attention and if you call in an excited, happy voice, your Beagle will come to you. The moment he reaches you, give him a tasty treat so he is instantly rewarded for making the 'right' decision.

The training line is very useful when your Beagle becomes an adolescent and is testing your leadership. When you have reinforced the correct behaviour a number of times, your dog will build up a strong recall and you

will not need to use a training line.

WALKING ON A LOOSE LEAD

This is a simple exercise but it does not come naturally to the Beagle. A Beagle tends to be distracted by the scents he finds en route and 'forgets' what he is meant to be doing. In most cases, owners make the mistake of wanting to get on with the expedition rather than training the dog to walk on a lead.

In this exercise, as with all lessons that you teach your

Beagle, you must make your training varied, offering a reward every now and then so your Beagle focuses on you and his mind is occupied with guessing when he is going to be given a treat.

- In the early stages of lead training, allow your puppy to pick his route and follow him. He will get used to the feeling of being 'attached' to you and has no reason to put up any resistance.
- Next, find a toy or a tasty treat and show it to your puppy. Let him follow the treat/toy for a few paces and then reward him.
- Build up the amount of time your pup will walk with you and when he is walking nicely by your side, introduce the verbal command "Heel" or "Close". Give lots of praise when your pup is in the correct position.
- When your pup is walking alongside you, keep focusing his attention on you by using his name and then rewarding him when he looks at you. If it is going well, introduce some changes of direction.
- Do not attempt to take your puppy out on the lead until you have mastered the basics at home. You need to be confident that your puppy accepts the lead and will focus his attention on you, when requested, before you face the challenge of a busy environment.
- If you are heading somewhere special, such as to the park, your Beagle will probably try to

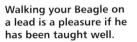

Walking your Beagle on a lead is a pleasure if he has been taught well.

pull because he is impatient to get there. If this happens, stop, call your dog to you and do not set off again until he is in the correct position. It may take time, but your Beagle will eventually realise that it is more productive to walk by your side than to pull ahead.

STAYS

This may not be the most exciting exercise, but it is one of the most useful. There are many occasions when you want your Beagle to stay in position, even if it is only for a few seconds. The classic example is when you want your Beagle to stay in the back of the

With practice, your Beagle will learn to "Stay" despite the distractions of other dogs.

car until you have clipped on his lead. Some trainers use the verbal command "Stay" when the dog is to stay in position for an extended period of time and "Wait" if the dog is to stay in position for a few seconds until you give the next command. Others trainers use a universal "Stay" to cover all situations. It all comes down to personal preference, and as long as you are consistent, your dog will understand the command he is given.

- Put your puppy in a 'Sit' or a 'Down' and use a hand signal (flat palm, facing the dog) to show he is to stay in position. Step a pace away from the dog. Wait a second, step back and

reward him. If you have a lively pup, you may find it easier to train this exercise on the lead, or you can try it at mealtimes and ask your Beagle to "Wait" a few seconds before putting his food bowl down.
- Gradually increasing the distance you can leave your dog. When you return to your dog's side, praise him quietly and release him with a command, such as "OK".
- Remember to keep your body language very still when you are teaching this exercise and avoid eye contact with your dog. Work on this exercise over a period of time and you will build up a really reliable 'Stay'.

SOCIALISATION

While your Beagle is mastering basic obedience exercises, there is other, equally important work to do with him. A Beagle is not only becoming a part of your home and family, he is becoming a member of the community. He needs to be able to live in the outside world, coping calmly with every new situation that comes his way. It is your job to introduce him to as many different experiences as possible and to encourage him to behave in an appropriate manner.

In order to socialise your Beagle effectively, it is helpful to understand how his brain is developing and then you will get a perspective on how he sees the world.

CANINE SOCIALISATION
(Birth to 7 weeks)
This is the time when a dog learns how to be a dog. By interacting with his mother and his littermates, a young pup learns about leadership and submission. He learns to read body posture so that he understands the intentions of his mother and his siblings. A puppy that is taken away from his litter too early may always have behavioural problems with other dogs, either being fearful or aggressive.

SOCIALISATION PERIOD
(7 to 12 weeks)
This is the time to get cracking and introduce your Beagle puppy to as many different experiences as possible. This includes meeting

different people, other dogs and animals, seeing new sights and hearing a range of sounds, from the vacuum cleaner to the roar of traffic. A puppy learns very quickly and what he learns will stay with him for the rest of his life. This is the best time for a puppy to move to a new home, as he is adaptable and ready to form deep bonds.

FEAR-IMPRINT PERIOD
(8 to 11 weeks)
This occurs during the socialisation period and it can be the cause of problems if it is not handled carefully. If a pup is exposed to a frightening or painful experience, it will lead to lasting impressions. Obviously, you will attempt to avoid frightening situations, such as your pup being bullied by a mean-spirited older dog, or a firework going off, but you cannot always protect your puppy from the unexpected. If your pup has a nasty experience, the best plan is to make light of it and distract him by offering him a treat or a game. The pup will take the lead from you and will be reassured that there is nothing to worry about. If you mollycoddle him and sympathise with him, he is far more likely to retain the memory of his fear.

SENIORITY PERIOD
(12 to 16 weeks)
During this period, your Beagle puppy starts to cut the apron strings and becomes more

independent. He will test out his status to find out who is the pack leader: him or you. Bad habits, such as play biting, which may have been seen as endearing a few weeks earlier, should be firmly discouraged. Remember to use positive, reward-based training, but make sure your puppy knows that you are the leader and must be respected.

SECOND FEAR-IMPRINT
PERIOD (6 to 14 months)
This period is not as critical as the first fear-imprint period, but it should still be handled carefully. During this time your Beagle may appear apprehensive, or he may show fear of something familiar. You may feel as if you have taken a backwards step, but if you adopt a calm, positive manner, your Beagle will see that there is

nothing to be frightened of. Do not make your dog confront the thing that frightens him. Simply distract his attention, and give him something else to think about, such as obeying a simple command, such as "Sit" or "Down". This will give you the opportunity to praise and reward your dog and will help to boost his confidence.

YOUNG ADULTHOOD AND
MATURITY (1 to 4 years)
The timing of this phase depends on the size of the dog: the bigger the dog, the later it is. This period coincides with a dog's increased size and strength, mental as well as physical. Some dogs, particularly those with a more assertive nature, will test your leadership again and may become aggressive towards other dogs.

Puppies learn important lessons from their mother and from their littermates.

The well socialised Beagle is calm and confident, and is happy to accept his place in the pack – be it human or canine.

Firmness and continued training are essential at this time, so that your Beagle accepts his status in the family pack.

IDEAS FOR SOCIALISATION

When you are socialising your Beagle, you want him to experience as many different situations as possible. Try out some of the following ideas, which will ensure your Beagle has an all-round education.

If you are taking on a rescued dog and have little knowledge of his background, it is important to work through a programme of socialisation. A young puppy soaks up new experiences like a sponge, but an older dog can still learn. If a rescued dog shows fear or apprehension, treat him in exactly the same way as you would treat a youngster who is going through the second fear-imprint period.

- Accustom your puppy to household noises, such as the vacuum cleaner, the television and the washing machine.
- Ask visitors to come to the door, wearing different types of clothing – for example, wearing a hat, a long raincoat, or carrying a stick or an umbrella.
- If you do not have children at home, make sure your Beagle has a chance to meet and play with them. Go to a local park and watch children in the play area. You will not be able to take your Beagle inside the play area, but he will see children playing and will get used to their shouts of excitement.
- Attend puppy classes. These are designed for puppies between the ages of 12 to 20 weeks and give puppies a chance to play and interact together in a controlled, supervised environment. Your vet will have details of a local class.
- Take a walk around some quiet streets, such as a residential area, so your Beagle can get used to the sound of traffic. As he becomes more confident, progress to busier areas. Remember, your lead is like a live wire and your feelings will travel directly to your Beagle. Assume a calm, confident manner and your puppy will take the lead from you and have no reason to be fearful.
- Take a walk through an outdoor market or visit a car-boot sale where there will be lots of people, children in pushchairs, plus a variety of different sounds and scents.
- Go to a railway station. You don't have to get on a train if you don't need to, but your

TRAINING CLUBS

There are lots of training clubs to choose from. Your vet will probably have details of clubs in your area, or you can ask friends who have dogs if they attend a club. Alternatively, use the internet to find out more information. But how do you know if the club is any good?

Before you take your dog, ask if you can go to a class as an observer and find out the following:
• What experience does the instructor(s) have?
• Do they have experience with Beagles?
• Is the class well organised and are the dogs reasonably quiet? (A noisy class indicates an unruly atmosphere, which will not be conducive to learning.)
• Are there are a number of classes to suit dogs of different ages and abilities?
• Are positive, reward-based training methods used?
• Does the club train for the Good Citizen Scheme (see page 113)?

If you are not happy with the training club, find another one. An inexperienced instructor who cannot handle a number of dogs in a confined environment can do more harm than good.

Beagle will have the chance to experience trains, people wheeling luggage, loudspeaker announcements, and going up and down stairs and over railway bridges.
• If you live in the town, plan a trip to the country. You can enjoy a day out and provide an opportunity for your Beagle to see livestock, such as sheep, cattle and horses.
• One of the best places for socialising a dog is at a country fair. There will be crowds of people, livestock in pens, tractors, bouncy castles, fairground rides and food stalls.
• When your dog is over 20 weeks of age, locate a training class for adult dogs. You may find that your local training class has both puppy and adult classes.

THE ADOLESCENT BEAGLE

It happens to every dog – and every owner. One minute you have an obedient, well-behaved youngster and the next you have a boisterous adolescent who appears to have forgotten everything he ever learnt.

Every dog is an individual, so it is hard to be precise as to the exact age a Beagle shows adolescent behaviour, but in most cases, male Beagles tend to mature quickly and will show interest in females from as early as five months. However, they will not be fully mature until 18-24 months; the age this happens often depends on particular bloodlines. In terms of behavioural changes, a male often becomes more assertive as he pushes the boundaries to see if he can achieve top dog status. In some cases, a male may become frustrated, and will hang on to your leg or try to 'hump' a cushion. If this happens, do not reprimand your dog; he is not being naughty, he is simply a prey to hormonal activity. The best plan is to distract his attention

It is not unusual for a Beagle to test the boundaries as he grows up.

not fully developed.

Adolescence can be a trying time for both dog and owner, but it is important to retain a sense of perspective. Look at the situations from the dog's perspective and respond to uncharacteristic behaviour with firmness and consistency. Just like a teenager, an adolescent Beagle feels the need to flex his muscles and challenge the status quo. But if you show that you are a strong leader (see page 90) and are quick to reward good behaviour, your Beagle will be happy to accept you as his protector and provider.

WHEN THINGS GO WRONG

Positive, reward-based training has proved to be the most effective method of teaching dogs, but what happens when your Beagle does something wrong and you need to show him that his behaviour is unacceptable? The old-fashioned school of dog training used to rely on the powers of punishment and negative reinforcement. A dog who raided the bin, for example, was smacked. Now we have learnt that it is not only unpleasant and cruel to hit a dog, it is also ineffective. If you hit a dog for

with a game or some training so you give him something else to think about.

A female can come into season from six months onwards – and have a season every six months or so thereafter. However, there are always exceptions to the rule, some coming into season earlier or later, and some having longer or shorter gaps between seasons. A female's behaviour will change when she is in season; she may become more 'clingy', not wanting to go far from your side. Alternatively, she may become withdrawn and want to be alone. Females Beagles are not fully mature until they have had their second season, and it is not advisable to spay until halfway through the cycle following the second season, i.e. three months after the second season. If it is done earlier, it can lead to incontinence, as the bladder is

A Beagle may try jumping up, demanding your attention.

The best strategy is to ignore your Beagle, and only give him attention when he has all four feet on the ground.

stealing, he is more than likely to see you as the bad consequence of stealing, so he may raid the bin again, but probably not when you are around. If he raided the bin some time before you discovered it, he will be even more confused by your punishment, as he will not relate your response to his 'crime'.

A more commonplace example is when a dog fails to respond to a recall in the park. When the dog eventually comes back, the owner puts the dog on the lead and goes straight home to punish the dog for his poor response. Unfortunately, the dog will have a

different interpretation. He does not think: "I won't ignore a recall command because the bad consequence is the end of my play in the park." He thinks: "Coming to my owner resulted in the end of playtime – therefore coming to my owner has a bad consequence, so I won't do that again."

There are a number of strategies to tackle undesirable behaviour – and they have nothing to do with harsh handling.

Ignoring bad behaviour: The Beagle is an energetic, high-spirited dog and a lot of

undesirable behaviour in youngsters is due to over-exuberance. A Beagle may jump up at you to get attention, particularly if you keep more than one dog and he is vying with other members of the 'pack'. If you tell him to get off or push him down, he is perfectly happy because he has got the attention he was seeking.

In this situation, the best and most effective response is to ignore your Beagle. Turn your back on him, do not speak to him and avoid all eye contact. The moment he has all four feet on the ground, reward him with lots of praise, making sure he does not try to jump up again. It will not take a clever Beagle long to realise that jumping up does not get him the attention he wants – he only gets this when he stays on the ground. In this way you have turned the tables; your Beagle is no longer 'training' you to do what he wants, you are in control and he is rewarded when he behaves in the way you want.

Stopping bad behaviour: There are occasions when you want to call an instant halt to whatever it is your Beagle is doing. He may have just jumped on the sofa, or you may have caught him red-handed in the rubbish bin. He has already committed the 'crime', so your aim is to stop him and to redirect his attention. You can do this by using a deep, firm tone of voice to say "No", which will startle him, and then call him to you in a bright, happy voice. If necessary, you can attract him with a toy or a treat. The moment your Beagle stops the undesirable

TAKING CONTROL

If you have trained and socialised your Beagle correctly, he will know his place in the family pack and will have no desire to challenge your authority. As we have seen, adolescent males may test the boundaries, but this behaviour will not continue if you exhibit the necessary leadership skills.

If you have taken on a rescued dog who has not been trained and socialised, or if you have let your adolescent Beagle become over-assertive, you may find you have a problem dog who is trying to take control. This is expressed in many different ways, which may include the following:
- Showing lack of respect for your personal space. For example, your dog will barge through doors ahead of you or jump up at you.
- Getting up on to the sofa or your favourite armchair, even though he knows this is not allowed.
- Ignoring basic obedience commands, particularly the recall.
- Showing no respect to younger members of the family, pushing amongst them and completely ignoring them.

- Male dogs may start marking (cocking their leg) in the house.
- Aggression towards people or other dogs (see page 109).

If you see signs of your Beagle behaving in this way, you must work at lowering his status so that he realises that you are the leader and he must accept your authority. Although you need to be firm, you also need to use positive training methods so that your Beagle is rewarded for the behaviour you want. In this way, his 'correct' behaviour will be strengthened and repeated.

The golden rule is not to become confrontational. The dog will see this as a challenge and may become even more determined not to co-operate. There are a number of steps you can take to lower your Beagle's status, which are far more likely to have a successful outcome. They include:
- Go back to basics and hold daily training sessions, making sure you have some really tasty treats. Run through all the training exercises you have taught your Beagle. By providing him with

behaviour and comes towards you, you can reward his good behaviour. You can back this up by running through a couple of simple exercises, such as a 'Sit' or a 'Down', and rewarding with treats. In this way, your Beagle focuses his attention on you and sees you as the greatest source of reward and pleasure.

In a more extreme situation, when you want to interrupt undesirable behaviour and you know that a simple "No" will not do the trick, you can try something a little more dramatic. If you get a can and fill it with pebbles, it will make a really loud noise when you shake it or throw it. The same effect can be

achieved with purpose-made training discs available from pet stores. The dog will be startled and stop what he is doing. Even better, the dog will not associate the unpleasant noise with you. This gives you the perfect opportunity to be the nice guy, calling the dog to you and giving him lots of praise.

things to do, you are giving him mental stimulation and you have the opportunity to make a big fuss of him and reward him when he does well. This will help to reinforce the message that you are the leader and that it is rewarding to do as you ask.

- Teach your Beagle something new; this can be as simple as learning a trick, such as shaking paws. Having something new to think about will keep his mind occupied and he will benefit from interacting with you.
- Be 100 per cent consistent with all house rules – your Beagle must never sit on the sofa and you must never allow him to jump up at you.
- You can reinforce your role as provider by dropping some extra treats in your Beagle's food bowl when he is eating. Someone who feeds him – and gives him extra treats – is worthy of respect.
- Do not let your Beagle barge through doors ahead of you or leap from the back of the car before you release him. You may need to put your dog on the lead and teach him to "Wait" at doorways and then reward him for letting you go through first.

If your Beagle is progressing well with his retraining programme, think about getting

A Beagle may try to elevate his status by breaking house rules.

involved with a dog sport, such as agility or flyball. This will give your Beagle a positive outlet for his energies. However, if your Beagle is still trying to take control, or you have any other concerns, do not delay in seeking the help of an animal behaviourist.

You may feel you are hearing too much of your Beagle's voice.

PROBLEM BEHAVIOUR

If you have trained your Beagle from puppyhood, survived his adolescence and established yourself as a fair and consistent leader, you will end up with a brilliant companion dog. The Beagle is a well-balanced dog, who rarely has hang-ups if he has been correctly reared and socialised.

However, it may be that you may have taken on a rescued Beagle that has established behavioural problems. If you are worried about your Beagle and feel out of your depth, do not delay in seeking professional help. This is readily available, usually through a referral from your vet, or you can find out additional information on the internet (see Appendices for web addresses). An animal behaviourist will have experience in tackling problem behaviour and will be able to help both you and your dog.

BARKING

The Beagle has a deep, sonorous bark –which is easier on the ear than a piercing yap – but you may still find it is a sound you are hearing too often.

A Beagle may bark for the following reasons:

- To get attention
- To demand his own way
- To lay claim to his territory – running along a boundary fence and barking when people pass by.

In the first two instances, barking can be cured by being

ignored (see page 103 Ignoring bad behaviour). A Beagle will be quick to realise that barking does not pay off and you can redirect his energies to more appropriate behaviour.

Barking to mark a boundary line is more likely to happen if you live in a rural location and passers-by have a novelty value. Try not to let his behaviour become habitual, as it will be far harder to remedy if it has become ingrained. The best plan is to expose your dogs to a wide variety of different situations, including visiting friends' houses, where your dog will not feel territorial and does not feel the need to react.

Beagles are notorious thieves – but you can train your dog to understand that he cannot take food without permission.

STEALING
Beagles are opportunists and will steal food if given half a chance. Never put any sort of bag on the floor (train friends and visitors as well), as it will be explored. That is why Beagles make such good detector dogs at airports (see page 21).

A Beagle can be taught to leave food – it is one of the tests in the more advanced Kennel Club Good Citizen (see page 109) – and this may help your Beagle to learn that he must seek permission before eating whatever he comes across. This is done in the following way:

- Start by asking your Beagle to "Sit" and kneeling in front of him. Let him see a treat in your hand.
- Close your fist, and when your Beagle tries to get the treat out of your hand, say "Leave", gently push him back and ask him to "Sit" again.
- Be firm, but as soon as he stops trying to get the treat – even if just for a few seconds – say "OK" and give him the treat with plenty of praise.
- Keep practising and you will be amazed at how quickly your Beagle learns that he will get the food if he leaves it.

- The next step is to put the treat on the floor, or on the edge of a chair, and as your Beagle goes to get it, say "Leave". He should pause, and, at this moment, pick up the treat and reward him with it. It may be better to have your Beagle on a lead to give you better control. Be firm and only reward him when he stops trying to get to the treat.

With practice, you will be able to stop your Beagle grabbing food that is dropped accidentally.

SEPARATION ANXIETY
A Beagle should be brought up to accept short periods of separation from his owner so that he does not become anxious. A new puppy should be left for short periods on his own, ideally in a crate where he cannot get up to any mischief. It is a good idea to leave him with a boredom-busting toy so he will be happily occupied in your absence. When you return, do not rush to the crate and make a huge fuss. Wait a few minutes, and then calmly go to the crate and release your dog, telling him how good he has been. If this scenario is repeated a number of times, your Beagle will soon learn that being left on his own is no big deal.

A Beagle should be brought up to accept time on his own without becoming anxious.

Problems with separation anxiety are most likely to arise if you take on a rescued dog who has major insecurities. You may also find your Beagle hates being left if you have failed to accustom him to short periods of isolation when he was growing up. Separation anxiety is expressed in a number of ways and all are equally distressing for both dog and owner. An anxious dog who is left alone may bark and whine continuously, urinate and defecate, and may be extremely destructive.

There are a number of steps you can take when attempting to solve this problem.

• Put up a baby-gate between adjoining rooms and leave your dog in one room while you are in the other room. Your dog will be able to see you and hear you, but he is learning to cope without being right next to you. Build up the amount of time you can leave your dog in easy stages.

• Buy some boredom-busting toys and fill them with some tasty treats. Whenever you leave your dog, give him a food-filled toy so that he is busy while you are away.

• If you have not used a crate before, it is not too late to start. Make sure the crate is cosy and train your Beagle to get used to going in his crate while you are in the same room. Gradually build up the amount of time he spends in the crate and then start leaving the room for short periods. When you return, do not make a fuss of your dog. Leave him for five or ten minutes before releasing him, so that he gets used to your comings and goings.

• Pretend to go out, putting on your coat and jangling keys, but do not leave the house. An anxious dog often becomes hyped up by the ritual of leaving and this will help to desensitise him.

• When you go out, leave a radio or a TV on. Some dogs are comforted by hearing voices and background noise when they are left alone.

• Try to make your absences as short as possible when you are first training your dog to accept being on his own.

If you take these steps, your dog should become less anxious and, over a period of time, you should be able to solve the problem. However, if you are failing to make progress, do not delay in calling in expert help.

AGGRESSION

Aggression is a complex issue, as there are different causes and the behaviour may be triggered by numerous factors. It may be directed towards people, but far more commonly it is directed towards other dogs. Aggression in dogs may be the result of:

- Assertive behaviour (see panel on page 104).
- Defensive behaviour: This may be induced by fear, pain or punishment.
- Territory: A dog may become aggressive if strange dogs or people enter his territory (which is generally seen as the house and garden).
- Intra-sexual issues: This is aggression between sexes – male-to-male or female-to-female.
- Parental instinct: A bitch may become aggressive if she is protecting her puppies.

It is very rare for Beagles to show any form of aggressive behaviour, and this would only occur if a dog were provoked. However, a Beagle has a long memory and if he is involved in a fight/attack instigated by another breed, he will remember the breed – any member of it – and not forgive.

NEW CHALLENGES

If you enjoy training your Beagle, you may want to try one of the many dog sports that are now on offer.

GOOD CITIZEN SCHEME

This is a scheme run by the Kennel Club in the UK and the American Kennel Club in the USA. The schemes promote responsible ownership and help you to train a well-behaved dog who will fit in with the community. The schemes are excellent for all pet owners and they are also a good starting point if you plan to compete with your

Beagle when he is older. The KC and the AKC schemes vary in format. In the UK there is a puppy foundation scheme followed by bronze, silver and gold levels with each test becoming progressively more demanding. In the AKC scheme there is a single test.

Some of the exercises include:
- Walking on a loose lead among people and other dogs.
- Recall amid distractions.
- A controlled greeting where dogs stay under control while their owners meet.
- The dog allows all-over grooming and handling by his

owner, and also accepts being handled by the examiner.
- Stays, with the owner in sight and then out of sight.
- Food manners, allowing the owner to eat without begging and taking a treat on command.
- Sendaway – sending the dog to his bed.

The tests are designed to show the control you have over your dog and his ability to respond correctly and remain calm in all situations. The Good Citizen Scheme is taught at most training clubs. For more information, log on to the Kennel Club or AKC website (see Appendices).

EMMA GOES FOR GOLD

Susan Arden, breeder of the Madika Beagles, proves that Beagles can be perfect canine citizens.

"The Kennel Club Good Citizen gold award is their highest award and a great achievement to pass, especially for a Beagle! Before attempting to pass the gold test, your dog must have already passed the bronze and then the silver tests. The bronze is very basic and most Beagles with some training should achieve this. That done, it's on to the silver; the biggest worry in this test is the food manners exercise. This is where the dog has to be on a loose lead in close proximity to someone who is eating – and not mug them! Once the silver test is passed, you are ready to train for gold. Fortunately, there is no time limit to these tests, so there is no rush if your dog isn't ready or simply not mastering what is asked for. The biggest

problem tends to be that once the Beagle knows what to do, will he choose to do it correctly in the test?

"My own Beagle, Emma (Barterhound Rosebud at Madika JW ShCM), despite being a very naughty baby, did excel at training class. She sailed through the puppy foundation scheme, and at only seven and a half months old she passed her bronze test. She was 11 months old when she passed the silver test and I was told then that the gold test would be held one month later!

"Fortunately, training for the gold doesn't just start after passing the silver; it is integrated into earlier training, as many of the requirements are similar for all the tests. Although I took Emma to training class once a week, I also did training at home. Beagles tend to get bored quite quickly, so I always keep training to a minimum, keep it fun, and I always end on a good point – even if I have

Emma resisting temptation in the Food Manners test.

had to go back to something really basic.

"I have never been so nervous as I was on gold test night; I felt ill. Emma is very unpredictable – she does tend to follow her nose – so anything can happen! The gold requires the dog to stop still on the way to you, which is very difficult, and there were a number of dogs who did, sadly, fail at this. Most owners shout 'Stop', but I used the command 'Wait', as Emma knew what this meant, as I use it out on walks: 'Wait' before crossing the road, 'Wait' for her lead to be put on, 'Wait' to be cleaned before going in the house. 'Wait' tends to mean 'hang on a second' – and it worked!

"The stay in and out of sight was easy to practise at home but still nail-biting on the night – would she still be where I left her when I came back in the room? Heeling off the lead, again, was something we had practised, so there were no huge worries with that, as she happily looks up at me as I talk to her while we walk round. Returning to the handler was straightforward enough, even with the distractions, likewise the 'isolation' section where the dog has to wait quietly when tied up, with handler out of sight, as I knew Emma would not get unduly worried about that.

"We did 'food manners' in the silver test and here it was again! Now that was a worry, as Emma is such a greedy, little dog; she never snatches food but taking it from a stranger is something else. Fortunately, she did remember her manners. 'Sending the dog to bed' can be difficult to teach and often needs a helper at the other end with a tasty treat, as the owner sends the dog away. I use a bit of carpet and Emma quickly associated that going to it meant getting a reward.

"Last, but just as worrying, was the general questions on the care and welfare of the dog. For example: How often do you worm your dog? What should you have with you when walking your dog? What would you do if you came across livestock? What would you do if your dog was sick? Although quite basic, the fear of getting anything wrong can make you unable to think. The relief on passing was enormous – I was absolutely delighted and amazed that Emma, at only 12 months old, did manage to get everything right on the night!"

An outstanding canine citizen: Emma with her bronze, silver and gold awards.

Showing is highly competitive – but it can be hugely rewarding.

SHOWING

In your eyes, your Beagle is the most beautiful dog in the world – but would a judge agree? Showing is a highly competitive sport, and, with entry fees and travelling costs, it can be quite expensive. However, many owners get bitten by the showing bug, and their calendar is governed by the dates of the top showing fixtures.

To be successful in the show ring, a Beagle must conform as closely as possible to the Breed Standard, which is a written blueprint describing the 'perfect' Beagle (see Chapter Seven). To get started you need to buy a puppy that has show potential and then train him to perform in the ring. A Beagle will be 'stacked' so that he stands in the correct show pose. He must gait for the judge in order to show off his natural movement, and he must also be examined by the judge. This involves a detailed hands-on examination, so your Beagle must be bombproof when handled by strangers.

Many training clubs hold ringcraft classes, which are run by experienced showgoers. At these classes, you will learn how to handle your Beagle in the ring, and you will also find out about rules, procedures and show ring etiquette.

The best plan is to start off at some small, informal shows where you can practise and learn the tricks of the trade before graduating to bigger shows. It's a long haul, starting in the very first puppy class, but the dream is to make your Beagle up into a Champion.

COMPETITIVE OBEDIENCE

This is a precision sport that tends to suit breeds such as the Border Collie, the German Shepherd Dog and some of the retriever breeds. However, there is no reason why you should not have a go and see how your Beagle gets on. The biggest obstacle is the retrieve, as Beagles are not natural retrievers and see

little reason for fetching a dumbbell, but you never know – your dog might prove them all wrong!

There are various levels of achievement, and the exercises get increasingly more demanding as you head up the classes. Marks are lost for even the slightest crooked angle noticed when the dog is sitting, and if a dog has a momentary attention lapse or works too far away from his owner in heelwork, again points will be deducted.

The exercises that must be mastered include the following:

- **Heelwork:** Dog and handler must complete a set pattern on and off the lead, which includes left turns, right turns, about turns and changes of pace.
- **Recall:** This may be when the handler is stationary or on the move.
- **Retrieve:** This may be a dumbbell or any article chosen by the judge.
- **Sendaway:** The dog is sent to a

designated spot and must go into an instant 'Down' until he is recalled by the handler.

- **Stays:** The dog must stay in the 'Sit' and in the 'Down' for a set amount of time. In advanced classes, the handler is out of sight.
- **Scent:** The dog must retrieve a single cloth from a pre-arranged pattern of cloths that has his owner's scent, or in advanced classes, the judge's scent. There may also be decoy cloths.
- **Distance control.** The dog must execute a series of exercises ('Sit', 'Stand', 'Down') without moving from his position and with the handler at a distance.

Even though competitive obedience requires accuracy and precision, ensure you make it fun for your Beagle, with lots of praise and rewards so that you motivate him to do his best. Many training clubs run advanced classes for those who want to compete in obedience, or you can hire the services of a professional trainer for one-on-one sessions.

AGILITY

This fun sport has grown enormously in popularity over the past few years, and the energetic Beagle is more than capable of competing to a high level. If you fancy having a go, make sure you have good control over your Beagle and keep him slim. Agility is a very physical sport, which demands fitness from both dog and handler.

In agility competitions, each

BEAGLES CAN DO AGILITY!

Through the tyre.

Down the A-frame.

Clearing the hurdles.

OLLIE'S STAR TURN

Sue Leader got involved with agility as a way of socialising her Beagle, Ollie, but soon they were hooked…

"We started agility training when Ollie, my Beagle, was 12 months old. Living in a remote location I wanted him to socialise with other dogs, and agility seemed a fun way to do this. Ollie was quick to learn; he is a bright, lively and intelligent dog with lots of energy and enthusiasm, especially if the reward for his efforts is food…

"Agility has also been an excellent bonding tool for me and Ollie; it is something we do together as a team, and it has also reinforced obedience training.

"Ollie's motivation for performing well at agility is food – his reward is a piece of sausage at the end of each course. We do have 'sniffy' days (where Ollie's nose is constantly on the ground) when rabbits have been on the training field. On these occasions the scent of a rabbit is far more important to him than my commands or a piece of sausage. These are frustrating days for me, but they come with the territory of owning a scent hound.

"We have been doing agility as a hobby with the same club for four years now and have won several rosettes, and even, on occasions, beaten collies!

"Ollie is not the fastest competitor – he prefers the dog walk and A-frame apparatus to the jumps, as he looks down on everyone from the top of these! But he is steady, accurate and obedient. Ollie loves doing agility – and so do I!"

dog must complete a set course over a series of obstacles, which include:
• Jumps (upright hurdles and long jump, varying in height – small, medium and large, depending on the size of the dog)
• Weaves
• A-frame
• Dog walk
• Seesaw
• Tunnels (collapsible and rigid)
• Tyre

Dogs may compete in Jumping classes, with jumps, tunnels and weaves, or in Agility classes, which have the full set of equipment. Faults are awarded for poles down on the jumps, missed contact points on the A-frame, dog walk and seesaw, and refusals. If a dog takes the wrong course, he is eliminated. The winner is the dog that completes the course in the fastest time with no faults. As you progress up the levels, courses become progressively harder with more twists, turns and changes of direction.

If you want to get involved in Agility, you will need to find a club that specialises in the sport (see Appendices). You will not be allowed to start training until your Beagle is 12 months old and you cannot compete until he is 18 months old. This rule is for the protection of the dog, who may suffer injury if he puts strain on bones and joints while he is still growing.

FLYBALL
The Beagle is not a natural retriever, but with training he can

enjoy the hurly burly and excitement of competing in flyball.

Flyball is a team sport; the dogs love it and it is undoubtedly the noisiest of all the canine sports!

Four dogs are selected to run in a relay race against an opposing team. The dogs are sent out by their handlers to jump four hurdles, catch the ball from the flyball box and then return over the hurdles. At the top level, this sport is fast and furious and although it is dominated by Border Collies, the Beagle can make a contribution. This is particularly true in multibreed competitions, where the team is made up of four dogs of different breeds and only one can be a Border Collie or a Working Sheepdog. Points are awarded to dogs and teams. Annual awards are given to top dogs and top teams, and milestone awards are given out to dogs as they attain points throughout their flyballing careers.

DANCING WITH DOGS

This sport is relatively new, but it is becoming increasingly popular. It is very entertaining to watch, but it is certainly not as simple as it looks. To perform a choreographed routine to music with your Beagle demands a huge amount of training.

Dancing with dogs is divided into two categories: Heelwork to Music and Canine Freestyle. In Heelwork to Music, the dog must work closely with his handler and show a variety of close 'heelwork' positions. In Canine Freestyle, the routine can be more flamboyant, with the dog working at a distance from the handler and performing spectacular tricks. Routines are judged on style and presentation, content and accuracy.

SUMMING UP

The Beagle is an outstanding companion dog – and once you have owned one, no other breed will do. He is intelligent, fun-loving, and loyal. Make sure you keep your half of the bargain: spend time socialising and training your Beagle so that you can be proud to take him anywhere and he will always be a credit to you.

BERTIE TAKES THE STAGE

Lucy Hankey, aged 13, has trained her Beagle, Bertie, to compete in heelwork to music competitions, and he certainly made his mark.

"Teaching Beagles heelwork to music is just as easy as teaching any other breed of dog. It is the Beagle's willingness to learn and love of food and rewards that allows you to teach your dog and train for this entertaining sport.

"Heelwork to music started with obedience heelwork and music playing in the background, but since then it has progressed to more complicated and crowd-pleasing moves and tricks. It is a highly competitive sport, but equally learnt for fun, and is very rewarding for both you and your dog. You will find not only that you are providing your dog with the great enjoyment and learning that he craves, but you're also building a great bond between you and your dog.

Continued on page 116...

Continued from page 115...

"In 2004, I was lucky enough to acquire my 'longed for' first Beagle, named Bertie, after saving my pocket money for two years and demonstrating to my parents that I was capable of the responsibility of owning a dog. We started breed showing and agility classes, but we still found that for Bertie, this wasn't enough. I discovered heelwork to music after seeing it on the TV at Crufts, and was inspired to have a go. I started training with the Blue Merle Clicker Academy and learned how to put routines together.

"Since then, I have been invited to do demonstrations at several events. I also qualified for and competed at Crufts in the heelwork to music final in 2010.

"To start training, you will need to teach your dog basic obedience (sit, stand, heel, and lie down). An effective way to train your dog to dance is to use the clicker method and be equipped with some nice, tasty rewards. Once you have built up the basic commands, you can start training the more interesting and advanced moves, such as the beg, roll over, and weaves. Remember, it's meant to be fun, so teach tricks one step at a time and reward your dog with lots of praise and some tasty treats. Good luck!

Bertie and Lucy.

Both paws on the pole

Taking a bow.

Ch. Nedlaw Barbarian.
Photo: Sue Domun.

THE PERFECT BEAGLE

Chapter 7

The perfect Beagle has yet to be bred, but it has given many people, who love this little hound, many years of pleasure striving for perfection. An interest in and understanding of construction and movement, with an equal interest in pedigrees, is the basis for many breeders who struggle to produce the perfect Beagle. I have been lucky enough to breed several Champions and even when I look at them I have to give a little sigh and think, "So near yet so far" for they have all had a little something I would like to improve upon.

THE INFLUENCE OF THE PACK BEAGLE

The early history of the show Beagle is closely shared with the pack hounds. Show and working hounds were once one and the same, for the better-looking pack Beagles were, in fact, those seen in the ring. The split between the show and working types scarcely existed; it was certainly not the wide gulf that it is today. The pack Beagle has always had a great variety of size and type. This has come about over many years when Masters of Packs bred to their own likes and dislikes. The first packs of Beagles were very often much smaller in size than we see today. Their hounds could be as small as 10-12 inches (25.5-30.5 cms) at the withers and would hunt rabbit, hare, fox and, indeed, even stoats or weasels. However, as the British countryside began to change between the 1700s and 1800s, and the land was turned to more cultivation, these little hounds struggled to hunt their quarry.

Their followers, too, wanted a sport that gave more of a challenge to crossing the countryside on foot, and many turned to riding and the excitement of jumping!

At the beginning of the 1800s, the numbers of Beagle packs went into a sharp decline. Indeed by 1850 there seems to have been only about a dozen known packs in existence. The Beagle itself had to change and a few good houndsmen set themselves the task of improving their little hounds. Gradually, over the next few years, the number of packs began to increase – and so did the size of their hounds. By the beginning of the 1900s there were more than 50 packs registered with the Masters of Harriers and Beagles Association (formed in 1891). It is fascinating to note that in the 1902-3 season, 44

The variation in size stems from the Beagle's working past.

packs registered the height of their hounds as follows:

- 5 packs under 14 ins (35.5 cms)
- 9 packs 14 ins to 14.5 ins (35.5-36.75 cms)
- 19 packs 15 ins to 15.5 ins (38-39.25 cms)
- 12 packs 16 ins (40.5 cms)

The reason for the variation was because different sizes of hounds suited different working terrains, and packs would favour a particular size, depending on their geographical location. The Masters of Harriers and Beagles Association later agreed a height limit of 16 ins (40.5 cms) and all Beagles are measured before being allowed in the ring at MHBA Hound Shows.

The development of the American Beagle was initially based on British imports, so it is not hard

to see how the two sizes, now recognised in the US, evolved. In the first American Standard, drawn up by the American English Beagle Club in 1884, the height clause was as follows:

HEIGHT. The meaning of the term "beagle", a word of Celtic origin, and in old English "Begele" is small, little. The dog was so named from its diminutive size. Your committee therefore, for the sake of consistency and that the beagle shall be in fact what his name implies, strongly recommended that the height line be sharply drawn at fifteen inches, and that all dogs exceeding that height shall be disqualified as overgrown and outside the pale of recognition.

The question of size has always been one that causes a great deal of discussion in the showing world. The British Kennel Club Standard now requires the Beagle

to be: "Desirable minimum height at withers 13 inches (33cm); desirable maximum height at withers 16 inches (40 cm)". However, the current American Standard states: "There shall be two varieties: thirteen inch – which shall be for hounds not exceeding 13 inches in height; fifteen inch - which shall be for hounds over 13 but not exceeding 15 inches in height. Any hound measuring more than 15 inches shall be disqualified."

Over the years the UK Standard has allowed the exhibitor some leeway in the height of the hounds that they show. However 'desirable' seems to sometimes stretch to nearer 17 inches (43 cms), which is really moving near to the size standard for Harriers.

WHAT IS A BREED STANDARD?

"A Breed Standard is the guideline which describes the ideal characteristics, temperament and appearance of a breed and ensures that the breed is fit for function. Absolute soundness is essential. Breeders and judges should at all times be careful to avoid obvious conditions or exaggerations which would be detrimental in any way to the health, welfare or soundness of this breed. From time to time certain conditions or exaggerations may be considered to have the potential to affect dogs in some breeds adversely, and judges and breeders are requested to refer to the Kennel Club website for details of any such current issues. If a feature or quality is desirable it should only be present in the right measure."

The above statement prefaces all the Breed Standards of the Kennel Club in the UK, but it can be applied to countries all over the world where the Beagle is bred and exhibited. It reminds all breeders and judges that the breed should be fit for its original function and certainly no exaggerations should be seen in the Beagle. Soundness of conformation and movement are obviously of the utmost importance in a hound. However, the head with the correct "mild and appealing" expression is a very important part of the Beagle and could be said to be 'the window to the Beagle's soul'.

The Breed Standard gives us a picture to hold in our mind's eye, so that breeders and judges have a pattern to aim for. However, there is still room for individual interpretation of this Standard. This, I believe, is good for the breed as a whole and gives us the opportunity for personal preferences still to fit in the required Standard. These slightly different interpretations of the Standard should not vary to any great degree, and the hounds themselves should all present a fairly level picture, both in type and conformation.

THE BRITISH BREED STANDARD
The Breed Standard as laid down by the Kennel Club has remained practically unchanged since the end of the 1800s when it was compiled by the Beagle Club and the Masters of Harriers and Beagles Association. Up until then, when the majority of

Ch. Chapscroft Briar: This bitch has a stunning show record in the UK which includes Best Puppy in Show, Hound Group winner at Windsor and Driffield, 15 Best of Breeds, and a tally of 20 Challenge Certificates (including Crufts 2007 and 2008).

Beagles were owned and bred by hunting packs, it was left to the individual Masters to decide which type of Beagle suited their hunt country and their own preference in looks.

The Kennel Club was formed in 1873 and it was only then that shows held under its control began to take place regularly. Eventually, all breeds were required to produce a Standard that then became the property of the Kennel Club. It is interesting to note that the Beagle Standard has had very few changes made to it since. The original Breed Standard contained a scale of

points, the total sum of which added up to 100 points. The head alone added up to 35 points, showing that, even then, the head and expression were considered a very important part of the Beagle. The points system in all breeds was dropped in the early 1900s.

In 1973 the Kennel Club overhauled all Breed Standards. In order to give each breed an identical format to follow, a system of headings was laid down and each breed now follows this pattern.

The first requirement of any Standard is to convey a vivid, instantly recognisable mental

Am. Ch. Springfield'N'Skyline's Big Shot (15ins): This dog was top-producing Beagle sire for 2006, 2007 & 2008, and top-producing hound for 2008. He has sired over 50 Champions, to date, with many still showing.
Photo: Tom DiGiacomo.

picture of the specified breed, and all Breed Standards now start with comments under the heading 'General Appearance'. Most of the changes in the Beagle Standard have been for clarification of the written word, and the breed has changed little in basic construction over the last century. The pack Beagle has gone in a slightly different direction over the last 100 years and is now much sharper in temperament and lighter framed all through; heads, too, are finer built. The show and pet Beagle has now a more laid-back temperament and is stronger made with more bone and substance. The head is less snipey with a stronger muzzle.

The latest round of changes by the Kennel Club, which took place early in 2010, saw no changes to the Beagle Standard other than a long-awaited clarification on colour. Now when a breeder registers a litter they can only choose a colour for each puppy from a list of recognised colours for the breed. Hopefully, we will no longer see such colours as 'fawn' and 'cream' allowed to be registered, which are certainly not colours that are ever seen in a true Beagle.

THE AMERICAN BREED STANDARD
The Beagle has had a long history in the USA. It was first recognised

in 1885 and was developed using imported working dogs from the UK. The Breed Standard that is currently in use was revised in 1957 and still retains its Scale of Points, evaluating the importance of the various characteristics. Interestingly, 25 points are allocated to the head properties, compared to 35 points in the British scale, which is no longer used.

There are those for and against the Scale of Points; it is certainly a useful guide for both judge and breeder, as you can see where the priorities should lie. However, it does not take into account the more intangible characteristics, such as the overall quality and balance of a dog, so it can, at best, only be seen as part of the picture.

As we have already noted, the major difference between the UK Breed Standard and its American counterpart is the clause on size.

THE FCI BREED STANDARD
The Federation Internationale Cynologique is the governing body for over 80 affiliated countries encompassing Europe, Scandinavia, South America, South Africa and most of the Asian countries. The policy is to use the Standard from a breed's country of origin, so in the case of the Beagle, the British Standard is followed.

ANALYSING THE BREED STANDARD
It will now be interesting to look at the Kennel Club Breed Standard and the American Breed

DK Ch. Sopwith Camel's Othello: A top winner under FCI rules.

Standard to interpret what is required for a 'perfect' Beagle and to highlight differences between the two Standards.

GENERAL APPEARANCE
KC
A sturdy, compactly built hound, conveying the impression of quality without coarseness.

AKC
A miniature Foxhound, solid and big for his inches, with the wear-and-tear look of the hound that can last in the chase and follow his quarry to the death.

The descriptions above give an instant picture of a robust but elegant little hound with substance and quality.

CHARACTERISTICS
KC
A merry hound whose essential function is to hunt, primarily hare, by following a scent. Bold, with great activity, stamina and determination. Alert, intelligent and of even temperament.

AKC
No description given.

The old KC Standard gave no definition of Characteristics or Temperament; the current Standard had a much clearer and fuller description. We are looking for a busy, happy dog, conveying strength and endurance on the move.

TEMPERAMENT
KC
Amiable and alert, showing no aggression or timidity.

AKC
No description given.

The combined statements of Characteristics and Temperament provide a really important description of a Beagle's attributes. Living as pack dogs, they needed to get on well with other dogs. Outgoing by nature, they should be pleased to meet new friends, whether human or canine. Any aggression or timidity should be heavily penalised, and any dog or bitch showing signs of either should most certainly not be bred from.

Temperament can, of course, be heavily influenced by a puppy's upbringing and the more socialisation the puppy has as a youngster, the more he is likely to have an even temperament and take everything in his stride.

The Beagle temperament is lively and alert at work, and soft and gentle at home.

Looking at the head, the impression should be powerful without being coarse.

HEAD AND SKULL

KC

Fair length, powerful without being coarse, finer in the bitch, free from frown and wrinkle. Skull slightly domed, moderately wide, with slight peak. Stop well defined and dividing length, between occiput and tip of nose, as equally as possible. Muzzle not snipy, lips reasonably well flewed. Nose broad, preferably black, but less pigment permissible in lighter hounds. Nostrils wide.

AKC

The skull should be fairly long, slightly domed at occiput, with cranium broad and full. Muzzle of medium length-straight and square-cut – the stop moderately defined.

Defects – A very flat skull, narrow across the top; excess of dome, muzzle long, snipy or cut away decidedly below the eyes, or very short. Roman-nosed, or upturned, giving a dish-face expression.

The head has always been well described in earlier Standards and it is clear that the skull should be clean but strong, and that the muzzle should never be fine or snipy. There should be an adequate chin, which should be square not pointed. The stop is quite clearly defined. Lack of stop completely spoils a Beagle's head and gives the hound an untypical expression.

EYES

KC

Dark brown or hazel, fairly large, not deep set or prominent, set well apart with mild, appealing expression.

AKC

Eyes large, set well apart – soft and houndlike expression, gentle and pleading; of a brown or hazel color.

Defects – eyes small, sharp and terrier-like, or prominent and protruding.

The eyes are such an important feature in a Beagle. That lovely, soft, melting expression when a Beagle looks at you is so much a part of the breed; there is no place for light or orange eyes with a hard expression. A black eye is equally foreign to this breed.

The position of the eyes is equally important and adds to the overall look of the head. Eyes that are too close together, or the wrong shape and size, are all faults that we must guard against. The correct eye shape is not totally round and tends towards almond-shaped. None of the past Standards, nor even the present one, mentions the haw of the eye – the third eyelid. It needs to be dark in colour if it is not to give the hound a rather worried expression.

Nowadays when we are required to be much more aware of health and fitness, we should want the eye rims of our Beagles to be reasonably tight; the lower lid drooping away from the eye and showing too much haw is equally incorrect.

EARS

KC

Long, with rounded tip, reaching nearly to end of nose when drawn out. Set on low, fine in texture and hanging gracefully close to cheeks.

AKC

Ears set on moderately low, long, reaching when drawn out nearly, if not quite, to the end of the nose; fine in texture, fairly broad-with almost entire absence of erectile power, setting close to the head, with the forward edge slightly inturning to the cheek, rounded at tip.

Defects – Ears short, set on high or with a tendency to rise above the point of origin.

All the past Standards are very clear that the ears should be set on low. This enhances the head and expression of the Beagle. When judging the Beagle, you should not ask the hound to prick his ears, as this will sharpen the whole head and you will lose the lovely softness that you want to see. The whole 'leather', as the ears are called, should be soft and

Ch. Nedlaw Barbarian. The ears are long with a rounded tip. *Photo © Sue Domun.*

pliable to the touch. Sometimes you can feel a ridge of cartilage running down the length of the ear and this is incorrect and undesirable.

It is the head – the expressive eyes and the ears – that together really give us the blueprint of the true Beagle. The head of a Beagle really sets him apart from all other breeds of hound and his endearing expression shows his love and devotion.

MOUTH
KC
The jaws should be strong, with a perfect, regular and complete scissor bite, i.e. upper teeth closely overlapping lower teeth and set square to the jaws.

AKC
Jaws – Level. Lips free from flews; nostrils large and open.

The description of the mouth was not included in the British

The jaws are strong and the teeth met in a scissor bite.

Standard before 1972; an omission probably brought about by the fact that the hound shows of the hunting fraternity do not check their hounds' mouths when they are shown.

The teeth should be strong, white, and fit with a smooth scissor bite, with the upper front set sliding down over the lower row. The jaw should be straight across and not crooked in any way.

NECK
KC
Sufficiently long to enable the hound to come down easily to scent, slightly arched and showing little dewlap.

AKC
Neck rising free and light from the shoulders strong in substance yet not loaded, of medium length. The throat clean and free from folds of skin; a slight wrinkle below the angle of the jaw, however, may be allowable.
Defects – **A thick, short, cloddy neck carried on a line with the top of the shoulders. Throat showing dewlap and folds of skin to a degree termed "throatiness".**

The neck is an important part of the outline/topline of a Beagle. When set on correctly, with a slight arch or crest, it should appear to run down to the back of the shoulder blades, giving a long, clean line.

The old Standards required the neck to be moderately long and

The neck is long and slightly arched; the shoulders are sloping, clean and muscular.

with the throat showing some dewlap. A play on words, you may say, but interesting nevertheless. The neck must be in proportion to the rest of the body, and be muscular and strong. A generous reach of neck is much to be desired but often goes with a slightly longer body.

FOREQUARTERS
KC
Shoulders well laid back, not loaded. Forelegs straight and upright well under the hound, good substance, and round in bone, not tapering off to feet. Pasterns short. Elbows firm, turning neither in nor out. Height to elbow about half height at withers.

AKC
Shoulders sloping, clean, muscular, not heavy or loaded – conveying the idea of freedom

The forelegs are straight and of good substance.

of action with activity and strength. Chest deep and broad, but not broad enough to interfere with the free play of the shoulders.
Defects – Straight, upright shoulders. Chest disproportionately wide or with lack of depth.
Forelegs – Straight, with plenty of bone in proportion to size of the hound. Pasterns short and straight.
Defects – Out at elbows. Knees knuckled over forward, or bent backward. Forelegs crooked or Dachshund-like.

The shoulders should be clean and sloping, enabling the hound to have great scope and freedom of movement. Forelegs should be well under the hound. Pasterns are short and straight, giving strength and bone right down to the feet. The most common fault

of a short upper arm will inhibit the correct movement. The elbows should fit closely to the sides of the brisket and should not protrude or swing outwards when moving.

BODY
KC
Topline straight and level. Chest let down to below elbow. Ribs well sprung and extending well back. Short in the couplings but well balanced. Loins powerful and supple, without excessive tuck-up.

AKC
Back short, muscular and strong. Loin broad and slightly arched, and the ribs well sprung, giving abundance of lung room.
Defects – Very long or swayed or roached back. Flat, narrow loin. Flat ribs.

The old Standards are all in agreement that the chest should be well let down to below the elbow and the ribs well sprung. This is important in giving the Beagle the necessary heart and lung room. It is also important that the ribs extend well back.

The Beagle should be compact but not boxy. A little more length than height enables the hound to move with athleticism and the ability to cover the ground all day with ease.

It is a definite weakness for the ribs to be short and the loin too long. This type of body in a working hound usually denotes a poor doer and a hound that will not stand as much work as his better-built brother.

The topline is straight and level.

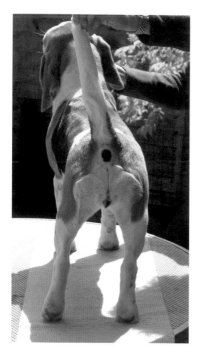

The hindquarters are strong and muscular.

HINDQUARTERS

KC

Muscular thighs. Stifles well bent. Hocks well let down and parallel to each other.

AKC

Hips and thighs strong and well muscled, giving abundance of propelling power. Stifles strong and well let down. Hocks firm, symmetrical and moderately bent.

Defects – Cowhocks, or straight hocks. Lack of muscle and propelling power.

The hindquarters should be well muscled but not out of balance with the forequarters. The term 'well let down' is applied to the length from the point of hock to the ground. If this part of the leg is too long, it could make the hound straight behind and it could cause the hound to move with a short and stilted action. The hindquarters are the 'engine room' and the driving force behind the movement of any working hound and therefore should be strong.

FEET

KC

Tight and firm. Well knuckled up and strongly padded. Not hare-footed. Nails short.

AKC

Close, round and firm. Pad full and hard.

Defects – Feet long, open or spreading.

The old adage 'no foot no horse' rings even truer for a hound's feet. The Beagle's feet should resemble those of a cat – tight, firm and well padded, not soft and spread.

TAIL

KC

Sturdy, moderately long. Set on high, carried gaily but not curled over back or inclined forward from the root. Well covered with hair, especially on underside.

AKC

Set moderately high; carried gaily, but not turned forward over the back; with slight curve; short as compared with size of the hound; with brush.

Defects – A long tail. Teapot curve or inclined forward from the root. Rat tail with absence of brush.

The tail is set on high and carried gaily.

ON THE MOVE

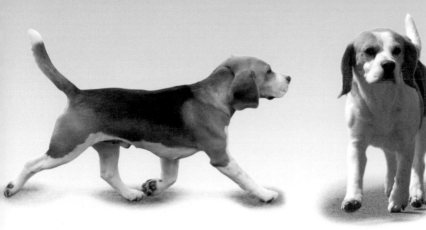

In profile, the Beagle has an even, lengthy stride. Photo: Gwen Ford.

The stride is free and long reaching from the front.

The drive comes through from the hindquarters.

The old British Standard makes it very clear that a well-carried stern finishes the picture of a "merry Beagle", and I can assure you that one of the pleasures of walking down a lane behind a pack of Beagles on exercise is the sight of all their waving sterns.

GAIT/MOVEMENT
KC
Back level, firm with no indication of roll. Stride free, long reaching in front and straight without high action, hindlegs showing drive. Should not move close behind nor paddle nor plait in front.

AKC
No description given.

In profile, the Beagle should show an even, lengthy stride, well balanced between front and rear. Moving 'up and back', he should move straight. Correctly angled construction and good muscle structure gives a good, free and forward-reaching, effortless stride. This is possible because the shoulders, elbows, hips, and stifles are properly placed and angulated, permitting free movement under the chest and loin.

COAT
KC
Short, dense and weatherproof.

AKC
A close, hard, hound coat of medium length.
Defects – A short, thin coat, or of a soft quality.

The Standard before 1972 states: "Smooth variety: smooth, very dense and not too fine or short. Rough variety: very dense and wiry."

Many years ago, there were certainly wire-haired Beagles. Whether these were purebred or had at some time in the dim and distant past been crossed with a terrier, we do not know, but they have certainly not been seen for many years.

COLOUR
KC
Tricolour (black, tan and white); blue, white and tan; badger pied; hare pied; lemon pied; lemon and white; red and white; tan and white; black and white; all white. With the exception of all white, all the

BEAGLE COLOURS

A blanket tricolour – not seen so frequently at present.

A faded tricolour

An open tricolour.

above mentioned colours can be found as mottle. No other colours are permissible. Tip of stern white.

AKC
Any true hound color.

As I mentioned earlier, this is the only change made to the British Standard in the recent overhaul of all Standards. The colours allowed are now all clearly listed so that a breeder, when registering a new litter, can only choose a colour from the above list.

One of the biggest changes in our Beagles over the last 50 years has been in the greater variety of colour seen in the show ring.

Years ago we only saw black blanket tricolours, and, occasionally, a lemon and white, or a tan and white. Nowadays we rarely see a true black blanket and are much more likely to find open marked tricolours or faded tricolours.

Some of the rare colour combinations, such as pied and pure white, are never seen at Kennel Club shows, although they do still appear in some pack Beagles. We still have some blue and tan mottled colours, which a few breeders have struggled to keep in the gene pool, and it would be a great shame to lose these old colours.

When judging we should always look through the large variety of colours and see the shape of the dog.

SIZE
KC
Desirable minimum height at withers: 33cms (13 ins).
Desirable maximum height at withers: 40cms (16 ins).

AKC
There shall be two varieties: Thirteen Inch – which shall be for hounds not exceeding 13 inches in height. Fifteen Inch – which shall be for hounds over 13 but not exceeding 15 inches in height.
Disqualification – Any hound measuring more than 15 inches shall be disqualified.

Tan and white.

Lemon and white.

The mottled colour is becoming increasingly rare.

Desirable is quite a long word and seems to cover several inches. However, do remember that Beagles are followed on foot when hunting. Unusually for a small-sized dog, the KC Standard allows us a large range in size of 7 cms (3 ins). There have been many good dogs and bitches that are well up to size. I think that a good guide is if the dog is well balanced and looks like a Beagle, not a small Foxhound, then it is acceptable even if slightly larger than one would wish.

FAULTS
KC
Any departure from the foregoing points should be considered a fault and the seriousness with which the fault should be regarded should be in exact proportion to its degree and its effect upon the health and welfare of the dog.
Note: **Male animals should have two apparently normal testicles fully descended into the scrotum.**

AKC
Faults are listed under each heading; a dog can be disqualified on size alone.

SCALE OF POINTS (AKC ONLY)

Head		
Skull	5	
Ears	10	
Eyes	5	
Muzzle	5	25
Body		
Neck	5	
Chest and shoulders	15	
Back, loin and ribs	15	35
Running Gear		
Forelegs	10	
Hips, thighs and hind legs	10	
Feet	10	30
Coat	5	
Stern	5	10
Total	**100**	*100*

SUMMARY
Success in the show ring requires commitment and an excellent Beagle. However, regardless of your dog's performance, remember that the best dog is always the one you take home.

HAPPY AND HEALTHY

Chapter 8

The Beagle comes in different sizes in different parts of the world, but all are characterised as medium-sized merry hounds who enjoy life to the full – and often live into their mid- to late-teens. The Beagle is generally a healthy breed if fed sensibly and given daily exercise to suit his lifestyle.

The Beagle is unique in being used for research and, as a result, have had many scientific papers written about their health. Many of the conditions listed in scientific books and papers are not found in the pet and show-owned Beagle, as the research population is different genetically. Those hereditary conditions that may be found in the normal pet and show Beagle population are discussed later and discussion is based on those most commonly reported as causing concern within the last few years rather than obscure or uncommon problems.

ROUTINE HEALTH CARE

As an owner, you should attend to routine preventative health care to keep your Beagle happy and healthy. It is important to check your Beagle for any abnormalities or changes; check ears, feet and the mouth as well as the skin for lumps or bumps. The Beagle has a nice, short coat, which does not hide much, so running your hands over your dog is a good way to check. Watch your dog's normal demeanour and question any changes, e.g. being quieter than normal or off his food – an unusual event for most Beagles!

DENTAL CARE

Keeping a dog's teeth clean reduces the likelihood of tartar building up and subsequent mouth infections and tooth loss. Every time a dog eats, some of the bacteria in the mouth passes into the bloodstream and can affect the kidneys and heart. Beagles are generally amenable to having their mouth checked and their teeth being brushed if needed. Pay particular attention to the canines and back molars, as these are the bigger teeth where tartar is most common, particularly since they do not sink so deeply into biscuits and chews when they are being eaten. A good diet and plenty to chew on will reduce this problem. There are dental chews on the market, and avoidance of a soft, mushy diet will help, but nothing beats regular, daily brushing.

NAIL CLIPPING

Nails should be kept short for the dog's comfort. There are several types of nail clippers available and the aim is to clip away any excess nail growth without touching the quick, which has a nerve and blood supply. If you are unsure, ask a veterinarian to show you where to cut and make sure you include dewclaws if the dog has any. A torn nail will require removal, as the dog will catch this on the ground every time he walks.

WEIGHT CONTROL

The Beagle is a greedy dog and will willingly eat more calories than he should. You ought to be able to just feel the ribs and note a waistline. Obesity will shorten your dog's life, as it will cause stress on the joints and heart. Feed a balanced diet, appropriate for your Beagle's age and exercise levels, and follow the guidelines as well as running your hands over your Beagle's body. Many of the commercial diets are generous

in their guidelines, so do not just "feed to the bag" but monitor your hound as well.

PARASITES

External parasites include fleas, ticks and mange mites. It is important to seek veterinary advice for treatment of the following parasites, as some are easier to eliminate than others.

    Internal parasites covered here will mainly include worms, with protozoal parasites coming under the Diarrhoea section later.

FLEAS

Fleas are very common and in the dog most are actually the cat flea, *Ctenocephalides felis*, which can live on either species. They only spend part of their life cycle living on the dog while they are gaining a blood meal; the rest of the cycle is spent in the environment, so control on all the dogs and cats in the house and their surroundings

is required. With the advent of central heating, fleas may be found all the year round, as they can survive in the warm house. Some dogs can be allergic to flea saliva, causing flea allergic dermatitis (FAD), so careful flea control will be required all the year around.

    The flea can carry one type of tapeworm eggs – *Dipylidium caninum* – so controlling the fleas will reduce this problem.

    There is a vast array of treatments, some of which can control all parts of the life cycle, so ask your vet which is most suitable for your Beagle.

TICKS

Ticks are more seasonal, as they spend part of their life cycle in rough, long grass and part on an animal for a blood meal. Ticks can carry a number of diseases, some causing serious illnesses that are rare or not present in the UK, which is why the PETS scheme requires a dog to be treated for ticks before re-entering the UK. If you are living or travelling outside the UK, it is very important to use tick preventatives, as your dog will not have met these diseases and will have no immunity. Some of the spot-on treatments control ticks as well as fleas, so good advice from your veterinarian will be helpful here.

    Removing ticks is easy, using one of the hook devices with a twisting motion. Do not pop the tick between your fingers but dispose of it carefully, as it may be carrying disease that can enter

It is your job to ensure your Beagle does not gain weight.

wounds on the human skin.

Ixodes ricinus is the most common tick in northern Europe and can carry Lyme disease, a bacterial infection caused by *Borrelia burgdorferi*, which mainly causes joint swelling and pain but can affect other organs. It is readily treated in the early stages with antibiotics, so it is worth consulting with your veterinarian if your dog has a tick bite or swelling where one has been. There is a vaccine available in the USA for Lyme disease and in areas where the incidence is high, it is worth using this as well as tick control to protect your dog.

There are many other varieties of ticks in different parts of the world and the main diseases to worry about are Babesiosis, Ehrlichiosis and Hepatozoonosis. All of these can produce serious disease and dogs travelling outside the UK are immunologically naïve and should be protected with tick preventatives such as a suitable spot-on or special insecticidal collars. The collars will also act against sand flies - see later.

Rhipicephalus sanguineus (also known as the red, brown or kennel tick) is an unusual tick, as it can complete its lifecycle indoors, being brought into the house on the dog and preferring to feed on them. It can reach

Dogs that hunt or are exercised in rural areas should be checked for ticks on a regular basis.

huge numbers within the house if not controlled, and although it can live outside in the warmer parts of the world, it does not survive the winter outside in the cooler regions. This carries Babesiosis and Ehrlichiosis and can be a significant vector of these diseases – mainly to dogs although occasionally to humans.

Dermacentor variabilis is an outdoor tick widely found in the USA. Its control is essential, as it transmits the human diseases Rocky Mountain spotted fever and Tularemi. In fact, it is not thought to be a major problem for dogs, as it does not cause them any disease issues, although it feeds readily on dogs as well as larger mammals, such as deer.

On the east coast of Australia the main worry is *Ixodes holocyclus* or the paralysis tick, which causes many fatalities in dogs and humans. Early treatment with anti-tick serum is necessary to prevent progressive paralysis and

death. The neurotoxin can be released by other tick species, but this is one of the main ones.

Dogs travelling into the UK (and into some European countries) under the PETS scheme must be treated for ticks 24-48 hours before re-entry. This must be carried out by a designated veterinary surgeon and the PETS passport stamped and dated.

Dogs from areas of the world where tick-borne disease is common and moving into areas where tick borne disease is uncommon may challenge the local dog population whose immune system is naïve to the disease and lead to problems. As travelling with pets is becoming more common, we must be careful not to expose them to disease they are not able to cope with and use local knowledge of dangers to help prevent problems. Tick control, both on and off the dog, is very important and may prevent a fatality. If ticks feed on dogs carrying disease, there is a possibility this will be transmitted to dogs that have never met the disease. Many of the diseases carried by ticks have been isolated in all species of them but not all seem to pass it on.

MITES
Mites come in many shapes and sizes; some are more contagious between dogs than others.

Cheyletiella or the 'walking dandruff' mite can make a dog very itchy (pruritic) and the skin is often flaky, which, combined with little white mites, gives a dandruff-looking appearance. This mite may bite people too, leaving little red spots on the skin. This is easily treated using Fipronil spray.

Demodex canis is a mite more often found in the skin in young dogs. It needs prolonged contact to be transmitted and may be passed during suckling in the litter from the mother. Many dogs have a few Demodex mites in the hair follicles on their skin without showing any signs at all, but it is thought that during periods of immune stress, the Demodex multiply and cause hair loss and thickening of the skin. The actual mite infestation is not itchy but there may be secondary bacterial infection, which causes the puppy to scratch. This needs specialised treatment often requiring amitraz baths weekly until the mites have all gone.

Otodectes is the ear mite and is characterised by a dog scratching its ears and having a brown waxy discharge. The mites are contagious between dogs and also cat to dog, so all pets in the household may need treatment. It requires a magnifying glass or otoscope to diagnose, but is easily treated with appropriate eardrops from your veterinarian.

Sarcoptes scabei, commonly called scabies, causes intense pruritis, particularly around the ear flaps and lower legs, leading to self trauma and secondary bacterial and malasezzia infection (leading to the dog smelling very 'yeasty'). The mites are contagious and may be passed from dog to dog or from foxes in the area. Rural Beagles are more likely to be affected due to the movement of foxes, but there are urban foxes as well now, so be on the lookout for this.

Trombicula or the harvest mite does not actually live on the dog for very long, but it causes intense itching, especially to the feet. They are red/orange in colour and can be seen with the naked eye.

SAND FLIES

Sand flies are not strictly parasites that live on the dog, but mention is made because they transmit a serious disease called Leishmaniasis, which can be fatal if untreated and is widely prevalent in some of the warmer parts of Europe and South America. Cases are turning up in the UK, and other areas where the disease was previously unknown, as dogs travel more widely abroad and rescued dogs are brought in from countries where the condition is endemic. Sand flies come out at night, so keeping the dog inside between dusk and dawn between May and October will reduce the incidence hugely. The special insecticidal collars mentioned for tick control are a really important way to help stop sand fly bites on your dog.

ROUNDWORMS

Roundworms are very common, with *Toxocara canis* found most often. They may be passed in faeces or vomited up and resemble spaghetti. The lifecycle includes small larvae passing around the body and spending some time lodged in the body

Mites can be highly contagious, spreading from dog to dog.

The bitch and her puppies should be treated for roundworm.

tissues. Most puppies have at least a few, as the larvae may cross the placenta and infect the pup before birth. Worming of the dam and puppies by the breeder will minimise the infestation, but as worm eggs are in the environment, it is essential to continue worming throughout the Beagle's life. Being a hunting and scent hound means the Beagle always has his nose to the ground and may continue to be re-infected.

Good hygiene, especially with children, is very important, as the eggs may hatch in humans, leading to larval migration in the body. So-called *aberrant larval migrans* can lead to cysts forming, such as in the eye, rarely causing blindness. Washing hands and

disposing of faeces when fresh will prevent this occurring.

TAPEWORMS

Tapeworms fall into two groups: those transmitted by fleas and those from rodents and small animals (such as rabbits). An infected dog will often be seen to have small, white, rice-grain-sized wriggly segments around the back end from those transmitted by fleas. The larger tapeworms are more common in those dogs that eat raw rabbits and rodents – Beagles can fall into this group!

In Europe the fox may carry *Echinococcus multilocularis*, which can infect humans causing serious disease. Thus, under the PETS travel scheme, dogs must be treated against this with

praziquantel 24-48 hours before re-entry into the UK.

HEARTWORM

Heartworm again falls into two groups. There is a worm called *Angiostrongylus*, which is an emerging parasite in the UK. Carried by slugs and snails, dogs can be infected by eating them or licking at the trails. There are very small slugs present in the UK, which can be found on grass when it is wet, and this is likely to be the most common route of infection when dogs chew on grass. The worm can damage the lungs or, rarely, lodge in the heart as well as causing clotting disorders.

The second type of heartworm – called *Dirofilaria immitis* – is not currently found in the UK or cooler parts of the world, as mosquitoes transmit it and the species involved is only found in the warmer areas. This may infect dogs travelling abroad from outside the range it lives in, so suitable preventatives to avoid this are available from your veterinarian and should be given before travelling and for a month after return. In some parts of the world this is a major problem and causes deaths in many dogs. It is important to use local knowledge and heed veterinary advice about control in these areas, as the adult worms can lodge in the heart and cause fatalities, as well as causing damage to other vital organs.

The first course of vaccinations is given to stimulate a puppy's immune system.

VACCINATION

There is an ongoing discussion about vaccination timing and how frequently boosters should be given after the initial puppy course. The puppy course is given to stimulate the body's immune system into producing antibodies against the diseases most prevalent in the country the dog lives in.

The core diseases we generally vaccinate against are: distemper, parvovirus, canine hepatitis, and leptospirosis. Some vaccines also contain coronavirus and parainfluenza. Other parts of the world vaccinate against Lyme disease and rabies.

PARVOVIRUS

Canine parvovirus comes in two forms: CPV1 and CPV2. CPV1 is a less virulent virus and its main effects are on puppies under three weeks, causing respiratory problems, and also during gestation, leading to foetal abnormalities and death. CPV2 is the more commonly seen of the diseases in the UK and the one found in vaccines. It is a relatively new disease, first appearing in the 1970s; it is very similar to the feline panleucopaenia virus and is thought to be a mutation of this disease. It spread rapidly worldwide once it appeared, which is why the vaccine is implicated and is now considered an important disease to control everywhere. It is usually rapidly fatal in

unvaccinated dogs – mainly young dogs are seen with it – although it is also found occasionally in older dogs.

When the disease first emerged it was seen in two forms, cardiac and intestinal. The cardiac form was seen in very young puppies born to bitches with no prior exposure or vaccination and caused myocarditis and death. Now it is more commonly seen as the intestinal form in older puppies (when maternal immunity has waned) or in unvaccinated young dogs, causing severe haemorrhagic diarrhoea and severe, persistent vomiting. Vaccination against this disease has fortunately reduced the incidence dramatically, but it is present in the environment and we should not be complacent about reducing vaccination.

DISTEMPER

Canine distemper virus (also known as 'hardpad' because of the extreme thickening of the foot pads it can cause) is a disease seen infrequently now that vaccination is commonly practised. It can cause a spectrum of disease from diarrhoea, vomiting and conjunctivitis through to neurological problems. Although not always fatal, it can leave a dog with seizures and in permanent poor health, being both thin and poor in coat.

HEPATITIS

Canine hepatitis, properly known as canine adenovirus 1, causes a range of symptoms, starting with nasal signs (such as coughing) and leading on to kidney and liver problems. During the course of the disease it may produce oedema (waterlogging) of the corneas, known as 'blue eye'. Vaccines usually contain CAV2, which is a more minor virus, causing respiratory signs, and produces good cross-immunity to CAV1.

LEPTOSPIROSIS

Leptospirosis is a bacterial infection. It is not present in all countries, hence not all countries vaccinate against it, but it is zoonotic, causing Weil's disease in humans. In the UK the two strains most commonly put in vaccines are *Leptospira interrogans* serogroups *Canicola* and *Icterohaemorrhagiae*. The former causes kidney problems and the latter jaundice. Both are generally fatal and can be contracted from the urine of wildlife, particularly rats.

KENNEL COUGH

There is also an intranasal vaccine against the two main causes of the **kennel cough syndrome** – *Bordetella bronchiseptica* and parainfluenza. The kennel cough syndrome can produce a range of signs, from a running nose to a retching cough, and there are several lesser infections, which can cause the syndrome. This is why vaccination helps reduce the incidence but cannot protect against every single cause.

RABIES

Rabies vaccination is a legal requirement in some parts of the world and owners must show their dogs are vaccinated according to intervals set by law. Some states in the USA, for instance, issue tags colour coded for different years and a dog not wearing one and caught straying may be euthanased without question. The incidence of rabies worldwide is variable and has been reduced in some areas by air dropping loaded bait, which, when ingested, vaccinates the wildlife population.

Rabies and the PETS travel scheme: It is possible to travel into the UK and in and around several European and 'safe' countries under the PETS travel scheme without your Beagle going through quarantine.

Routine boosters against rabies are required and the protocol must be strictly followed to ensure the dog has an up-to-date passport or entry may be refused. The PETS scheme is not fully standardized, so each country should be considered separately and the appropriate consulate contacted.

ANNUAL BOOSTERS

These serve two important purposes: the vet will give the dog a full health check and also give a vaccination against several of the most common diseases. Many vaccine companies have now done work on the duration of immunity, with some diseases offering protection longer than one year, and the booster vaccinations reflect this, with different components given at different intervals.

The PETS passport scheme means that show dogs can compete internationally.

GENERAL CANINE AILMENTS

ANAL GLANDS

These are scent glands found just inside the anal passage and continually secrete a liquid, which dogs use for marking territory when passing faeces. These may become impacted and sometimes form an abscess that bursts. Any discomfort will make the dog sit down and scoot, turn around and look at his back end or chew around the area. It is appropriate to empty them on such occasions, but emptying them too frequently may discourage the normal evacuation process.

ARTHRITIS

This is usually seen in the older Beagle and is due to general wear and tear on the joints. Beagles will often get stiffer as they age, with the elbows and hips mainly affected. In some dogs this may be due to hip dysplasia (see later) and can occur in a younger dog. Keeping your Beagle slim and routinely exercised is essential for joint and general well-being and will ensure he can continue to exercise into his teens. If your Beagle seems to be reluctant to go on a long walk or is stiff the day after exercise, consult the veterinary surgeon, as there are many ways to help enhance the older Beagle's quality of life.

DIARRHOEA AND VOMITING

Infectious agents or inappropriate eating in the Beagle may cause these conditions. Beagles are by nature greedy dogs and will pick up unsuitable things to eat and scavenge. As a breed they often seem to cope well with this behaviour, but at some stage of their life will either have diarrhoea and/or vomiting from doing this. In most cases it is appropriate to starve the dog of food for a short period and have controlled access to water, i.e. small and frequent laps rather than a bowlful. If the vomiting and diarrhoea settle, the dog may be given small amounts of the usual diet, gradually bringing back to normal over a couple of days. However, if the dog vomits continually or brings up or passes blood, the veterinary surgeon should be consulted. It is not uncommon to find that a Beagle has eaten something that causes a blockage and may even need surgery for removal of the foreign body.

There are some infections that affect people, too, namely Giardia, a protozoal parasite, which lives in the gut wall, and Campylobacter, both common causes of recurrent diarrhoea in dogs. It is important to be hygienic when interacting with your dog and to wash hands well. Isospora (also known as coccidiosis) is another protozoal

Arthritis is more likely to affect the older dog.

infection, which is mainly a problem for young dogs, under six months, causing diarrhoea. Adults usually develop immunity, although they can still pass it on.

EAR PROBLEMS

These are quite common in Beagles because they follow scents on the ground. They may get foreign objects, such as grass seeds, in them, or pick up mites while sniffing along the ground. Beagles are not especially keen on swimming but some may paddle in streams and puddles, also exposing the ears to sources of infection due to getting water in them.

If your Beagle is shaking his head a lot or scratching his ears, do check them. If they are red, sore or have an excessive discharge or smell, they will need veterinary attention.

LIMBER TAIL

Also known as 'limp tail' and 'Beagle tail', it is not unique to Beagles. The dog will be unable to raise the tail and may yelp out when the tail is examined. It is thought to be the result of whiplash when a dog shakes violently, such as after bathing or swimming. Originally it was thought that water had got into the tail, but it is most likely that the violent shaking of the tail bruises the nerve and muscle supply, and stops the tail being lifted.

Usually this will only last a day or so, but if it persists, it may require anti-inflammatories from the vet. If this occurs, it is also worth checking your dog's anal glands, as pain in this area may prevent the Beagle holding his tail as high as normal.

LUMPS AND BUMPS

These can arise in the skin for all sorts of reasons. Some may be benign and some more serious. Sometimes an allergic reaction will produce raised areas on the skin similar to hives in people. If this occurs, think about the possible differences in the last 24 hours, such as different foods, treats, titbits and environment changes (such as air fresheners). If in doubt, it is better to have a veterinarian check and find it is nothing to worry about than leave it until it is too big to address.

REVERSE SNEEZING

This is the colloquial term used to describe a dog that stops suddenly when exercising and appears to be struggling to get his breath. The two main causes are a conformational defect (an overlong soft palate, where the last part of the roof of the mouth impinges on the opening to the trachea) and allergic problems. Allergies in dogs rarely show as respiratory signs, such as asthma in humans, but this may occur, particularly in dusty weather or when a dog is exposed to high pollen levels. Persuading the dog to swallow a mouthful of water or a treat, or gently pinching the nose and stroking the throat usually stops this.

SKIN DISEASE

This can have many causes, for instance some of the external parasites mentioned previously, exposure to things such as nettles, or allergens. Hair loss,

Check your Beagle's ears regularly for any signs of infection.

141

The Beagle is a breed without exaggeration and is relatively free from hereditary disorders.

excessive scratching or any kind of skin lesion should be attended to for the dog's comfort.

Some dogs can develop allergic skin disease after exposure to certain things such as dust mites, flour or biscuit mites or certain plants. It is rare to find a very young dog, less than 12 months of age, with this, as most need prolonged exposure to react. So if a young dog has some skin problems, parasites should be ruled out first. Remember, the ear is also lined by skin, so ear problems may also be related to skin allergies.

Irritation and also cysts can occur between the toes. Again, grass seeds can cause this or small thorns working their way through the skin may also affect feet, causing an abscess. Skin disease can also occur in Beagles that have hypothyroidism (see under Genetic Diseases).

HEREDITARY OR SUSPECTED GENETIC DISEASES

CHERRY EYE

This occurs most commonly in the brachycephalic or flatter faced breeds, but for some reason the Beagle sometimes seems to be afflicted. Behind the third eyelid is a small gland known as the nictitans gland, which may become swollen and pop over the top of the third eyelid, giving the impression of a small red cherry in the corner of the eye.

The gland can sometimes be gently pushed back but may require surgery to stay in place. Some surgeons recommend removal if it continues to be a problem; the original theory that removal may lead to 'dry eye' through reduced tear production is now disputed, as the other glands in the eye produce enough tears.

EPILEPSY

This is a disease characterised by seizures involving involuntary muscle movements. The seizures may be partial or *petit mal* (involving, for example, one leg only), or *grand mal* (involving the whole body where the dog loses consciousness for a period of time). Epilepsy has been reported in the Beagle for a long time, probably originating in the packs from whom the breed is descended, and the level seems to be steady – with similar numbers reported each year.

The disease is under investigation in other breeds in terms of its suspected hereditary nature, including the type known as Lafora's epilepsy, which is often not responsive to drug therapy and difficult to deal with. This particular type is reported in a small handful of breeds, including the Beagle. Seizures may be caused by a large number of things, so a careful discussion with your veterinarian and recording of the seizures is important to decide on the true cause.

HIP DYSPLASIA

This is a condition where the hip joint has not formed correctly. The problem may be with the socket, which is part of the pelvis, and/or the femoral head, which is the top of the femur or thighbone. The joint should be a snug ball and socket so that the joint rotates comfortably and smoothly. If there is malformation, the joint is lax and abnormal pressure on the developing bone leads to an abnormal shape. The body continually remoulds and lays down bone in the joint, leading to arthritis and discomfort.

In big or overweight dogs this can be a major problem. But in the Beagle it may be overlooked, as they are light enough to cope. The condition has been studied at length in larger breeds of dog and is considered to be a product of genetics, environment and upbringing. No scientific studies have been done in the Beagle, but breeders in the USA feel that breeding from affected Beagles can produce affected offspring, so dogs diagnosed with the condition are best not bred from. There are different schemes in many countries for screening Beagles and these can be used by breeders as tools to prevent breeding from affected stock.

FACTOR 7 DEFICIENCY

This is reported in the USA and it is possible that the condition also occurs in the UK. It causes a mild bleeding disorder in most cases, and intermittent bloody diarrhoea has been recorded in Beagles that have been tested as affected. There is a DNA test available and the condition is inherited as a simple recessive gene. This means a dog may be clear (carry no copies of the gene), a carrier (have one copy of the gene and a normal one), or affected (carry two copies of the gene).

METABOLIC HORMONE IMBALANCES

I have included these in a group, as there are several hormones that can be secreted in too small or high an amount and upset the metabolism in dogs. Some may be hereditary.

Hypothyroidism, or an underactive thyroid gland, leads to an overweight, lethargic Beagle with a poor coat. The heart rate is slow, fertility may be decreased, and the whole metabolism is slowed down. This condition is considered by some to be hereditary, so it would be wise not to breed from affected dogs. The body produces antibodies to the thyroid hormone proteins and bonds within the thyroid gland. This condition can be tested for and treated with lifelong thyroid supplements.

Hyperadrenocorticism, or Cushing's disease, is caused by an over-secretion of the body's own cortico-steroids from the adrenal glands, by a failure in the control pathway; although the condition can also be induced by using the synthetic form of the drugs. This results in a pot-bellied dog with a thin coat and a tragic expression. The disease can be treated but not cured in the natural form, but if caused by taking cortico-steroids is potentially reversible once the drug is withdrawn.

Hypoadrenocorticism, or Addison's disease, on the other hand, is an under-secretion of mineralo-corticoids. This can be a life-threatening condition and should be treated carefully. Affected Beagles cannot cope with stresses and may collapse and die if not treated quickly.

MUSLADIN-LUEKE SYNDROME AND DWARFISM

These two conditions were originally linked but have now been reclassified into two separate inherited disorders.

Musladin-Lueke Syndrome (MLS) is named after the two Beagle breeders who did most work on the disorder and is also known as Chinese Beagle Syndrome. There is now a DNA test available for this and the condition has been found to be a simple recessive gene. The disorder produces Beagles with short toes on the front legs, and sometimes all four, so that they walk with an upright gait like a ballerina. They have a flatter skull shape with slanted eyes; high-set ears, and ear folds, although these may also be found in dogs that test normal for the condition. DNA-tested affected dogs should be kept out of the breeding pool. The DNA test can be used to identify Beagles carrying the gene and as long as they only have one gene copy, they can be bred to dogs that are normal, so no affected puppies are produced. For more information and DNA results from around the world, visit the international website www.salenko.co.uk/MLS.

Dwarfism is a form of chondrodystrophy, which means

Breeders work tirelessly to eliminate inherited diseases from their breeding programmes.

the bones (mainly long bones) grow abnormally and the limbs end up curved and foreshortened. There are breeds where this trait has been selected in a mild form, and sometimes people have inadvertently selected for it when breeding from smaller dogs to keep size down. The legs are bowed and the dog may also have abnormal vertebrae, leading to a short neck and hunched back. Such dogs may suffer skeletal pain and need medication to keep them pain free. Severely affected dogs have a short life span, but with a caring owner they may have a good quality of life. This is a hereditary disorder and such dogs should not be bred from.

SPINAL DISEASE

This is often listed as a disease that may affect Beagles. There are other breeds more commonly affected, but Beagles may suffer from disc disease when the intervertebral discs between the vertebrae (bones) of the spine deteriorate and push into the spinal canal. These cause pain at the least, and paralysis at worst. The condition can be slow or sudden, and any dog walking with a hunched back or problems with the hind legs should be checked.

STEROID-RESPONSIVE MENINGITIS (SRM)

Also known as Beagle pain syndrome, stiff Beagle disease, this is a disease currently under investigation for a possible hereditary link. It is not unique to the Beagle, being found in other breeds too, but the breed is over-represented compared to the general dog population.

The condition is most commonly found in young Beagles of 8-18 months, and is characterised by a general lethargy, stiff-legged gait, reluctance to eat or drink (much due to discomfort), and the Beagle may also have pyrexia (high temperature). The symptoms are caused by an inflammation of the blood vessels supplying the meninges (lining of the brain), and are caused by the immune system over-reacting. At

With good care and management, your Beagle should live a long, happy and healthy life.

the moment the cause is unknown. Treatment involves high doses of cortico-steroids and sometimes other drugs to suppress the immune reaction. Untreated, this disease can, in rare cases, lead to seizures due to scarring in the brain.

TUMOURS
The two most commonly reported tumours in Beagles are lipomas and mast cell tumours (MCT). Lipomas are really inappropriate deposits of fat, which grow most commonly in overweight Beagles. Even if the dog is dieted, they remain, and although they may be unsightly, it is uncommon for them to be malignant. Removal is gauged on whether they affect the dog or are large and heavy.

Mast cell tumours can be defined as benign, and then called a histiocytoma, which are more common in young dogs and usually self resolve if given long enough. Malignant mast cell tumours vary in grade but it is important to discuss with your veterinary surgeon the best treatment options, as they can lead to serious disease if not addressed correctly.

The author is indebted to Darlene Stewart of the Aladar Beagles for the information on MLS, dwarfism and Factor 7 as the Chair for the National Beagle Club of America Health Committee. Beagle problems in the UK may be reported to Mrs Sam Goldberg (Molesend Beagles) the KC Health Co-ordinator for the UK Beagle Clubs.

SUMMING UP
With good, informed care your Beagle should live a happy and long life. On the whole, the breed is healthy and fit and should live to a ripe old age.

BEAGLE

THE CONTRIBUTORS

THE EDITOR:
ANN PHILLIPS (LANESEND)
Ann has owned Beagles since 1964, when she bought a four-year-old retired brood bitch from the kennels where she was working, purely as a pet, and she has much to answer for! Ann registered her Lanesend affix with the Kennel Club in 1967 and began showing her trio of Beagles. She bred her first litter in 1968 and Jolyon (Ch. Lanesend Tallarook JW) was born in 1969. She bred several CC and Junior Warrant winners in the seventies and eighties, before cutting back to one house Beagle for the next twenty years, due to family commitments. Ann continued to judge and attend shows during this time and has judged the breed at Championship level since 1978, including Crufts in 2002 and the Beagle National in Melbourne, Australia in 2003.

Ann is an assessor for the breed at both shows and seminars. She was elected a member of the Kennel Club in 1998 and presently serves as Beagle representative on the Kennel Club Breed Liaison Council. She has the honour to be President of the Beagle Association, a post which she has held since 1985. Ann also writes the Beagle Breed Notes for the weekly canine paper *Our Dogs*.

Ann resumed showing Beagles in 2005 with the arrival of Stoker (Lanesend Nedlaw Admiral JW). She imported an Australian Champion, going back to Tallarook, in 2007 and his grand-daughter in 2010.
See Chapter One: Introducing Beagles.

DAVID WEBSTER (WEBLINE)
David Webster and his wife acquired their first Beagle, Letton Glitter, to found the Webline Beagles in 1958, eventually making up an International Champion and six UK Champions. David became a Championship judge in 1967; he has judged in many parts of the world and at prestigious shows such as the World Championship Show (1973), the European Championship Show (1983) and Crufts (1985).

He emulated *The Man Who Came to Dinner* by agreeing to become secretary of The Beagle Club for six months but stayed in that office for 26 years! He has been a Kennel Club accredited trainer of judges and has written Beagle breed notes for a weekly canine journal since 1965.

David has been a member of the Kennel Club since 1979 and is currently the President of The Beagle Club. He also has a keen interest in another breed, English Springer Spaniels, being President of The Southern English Springer Spaniel Society.
See Chapter Two: The First Beagles.

BRIAN FOSTER (STORMPASTURE)
Brian was bought a Beagle by his parents in 1970 and has never been without one since – his parents had Yorkshire Terriers but Brian wanted a 'proper' dog! As well as breeding many Beagle Champions, Brian has had success in other breeds, too. He has bred or owned Champions in Cocker Spaniels, Welsh Springer Spaniels and Boston Terriers, and has had winners in Petite Basset Griffon Vendeen and American Cockers. He feels this gives him an overview of the differences between the various breeds and their unique qualities. The Stormpasture Beagles have always made their mark in the ring, but Brian believes that not only should a Beagle be beautiful, it should also be fit and healthy and have an outstanding temperament.

Judging abroad in Denmark, Germany and the Czech Republic, has led to Brian bringing some of the old British lines back to England in the shape of Ch. Super Capricorn of Laurins Empire at Stormpasture who is known for his outstanding free movement which is so essential in the breed. Brian hopes that increased communication between Beaglers via the Internet will lead to more co-operation and understanding, as well as widening the gene pool for the betterment of the breed worldwide. He thanks the Beagles he has owned for giving him a richer, more exciting life than he could have ever wished for.
See Chapter Three: A Beagle for your Lifestyle.

JOAN LENNARD (BUTTEROW)
As a farmers daughter, Joan grew up with animals on the family farm. Her love of hounds grew from following foxhounds and seeing them work. In 1972, now married to her husband Keith and looking for a family pet, she decided on a Beagle and has owned and loved them ever since. Joan and Keith bred their first litter in 1974 when they registered their prefix 'Butterow'.

In 1979 Joan bred Ch. Butterow Crafty Chantress of Jesson (owned and campaigned by Honor and Jesper Eades). She became a Champion at just 15 months and won best of breed at Crufts in 1983.

Joan has always been concerned about the welfare of the breed and was privileged to become the first Secretary of 'Beagle Welfare' in 1979, helping to establish it as the national breed rescue organisation over the next few years. She was honoured to be made Patron in 1989 and has continued to support Beagle Welfare as much as she can.

Joan started judging in the early 1980s, but became more active in the 1990s, when she bought a new puppy to show. She started breeding the occasional litter at this time.

Joan became Secretary of the Beagle Association In 2005 and awarded Challenge Certificates for the first time in 2010.
See Chapter Four: The New Arrival.

PENNY CARMICHAEL (KERNEBRIDGE)
Penny has been involved with Beagles since the 1950s when her parents bought their first Beagle from Mrs Joan Beck. She registered her affix in 1969 and showed her dogs with some success, combining this with being mother to four daughters. In the 1970s she bred and campaigned two Champions, Ch. Kernebridge Young Jolyon and Ch. Kernebridge Trooper. She joined the Beagle Club working section and several of her hounds gained working certificates. Penny was chairman of the trustees of Beagle Welfare for some 10 years and has judged the breed in the UK and overseas. Penny is actively involved with the Beagle Association, and was elected a member of the Kennel Club in 2003.
See Chapter Five: The Best of Care.

PATRICIA SUTTON (ROSSUT)
Patricia has been involved with Beagles and many other breeds since the mid 1950s when her parents began the world-famous Rossut kennels. Her parents ran Windsor and Richmond Championship Shows for many years so Patricia has been involved in the world of Pedigree Show Dogs for most of her life. In the last 20 years she has continued breeding and showing Beagles and has made up many more Champions. She has bred four consecutive generations of Champion bitches and in 2010 made up two more bitch Champions. She continues to follow in her parents footsteps with her involvment

at the Kennel Club, and she sits on the General Committee, the Show Executive Committee and the Judges Sub-Committee, as well as being a member of the Training Board.
See Chapter Seven: The Perfect Beagle.

JULIA BARNES
Julia has owned and trained a number of different dog breeds, and has also worked as a puppy socialiser for Dogs for the Disabled. A former journalist, she has written many books, including several on dog training and behaviour. Julia is indebted to Ann Phillips (Lanesend) for her specialist knowledge about Beagles.
See Chapter Six: Training and Socialisation.

SAMANTHA GOLDBERG BVSc BSc(Hons) MRCVS
Sam bought her first Beagle in 1985, and then went through veterinary school, qualifying in 1992. She is the Kennel Club health coordinator for all the nine Beagles clubs in the UK and, as such, collates records and raises health concerns with the KC. She started working in a mixed farm and small animal veterinary practice but now work as joint head vet in a small animal only practice in the north of England, which also has a referral practice. Sam judges Beagles in the UK at Championship level and continues to show and breed Beagles, with a special interest in the less common colours.
See Chapter Eight: Happy and Healthy.

US CONTRIBUTORS

MARCY ZINGLER (US CONSULTANT)
Marcy L. Zingler was Senior Editor at Howell Book House before joining the AKC staff as Corporate Project Manager. One of her primary responsibilities was as Project Editor for the award-winning AKC 125th Anniversary book. As a freelancer, she was the only outside editor to work on *The AKC Complete Dog Book*, 20th Edition and 19th Revised.

Marcy's forty-year participation in the dog sport has included breeding, exhibiting, judging, and active leadership in national clubs as officeholder, AKC Delegate and Judges' Education Chair. A three-time National Specialty judge in her original breed, other assignments have included the AKC Eukanuba National Championship in addition to judging overseas and across the US.

Now semi-retired, in addition to judging, she again serves as a Delegate to the American Kennel Club.

LORI NORMAN (LOKAVI)
Lori Norman (Lokavi) has been exhibiting Beagles for 45 years, first as a handler, and then as a breeder/handler. Lori and her mother, Carol, have bred over 300 AKC Beagle Champions, as well as some abroad.

In the past five years, Lori has bred two bitches who became National Beagle Club of America's Dam of the Year (2005 and 2007). Two others were among the top five dams in 2006 and 2009. Lori co-bred the number two 15" Beagle in 2005, who remained in the Top Ten for four years, then bred a 13" Beagle ranked in America's Top Ten in 2008. One of Lori's stud dogs has been among the top five for three of the past four years. Show Beagle Quarterly magazine has ranked Lori and Lokavi among the top five American breeders, and top five American show kennels for each of the past five years.

USEFUL ADDRESSES

KENNEL & BREED CLUBS

UK
The Kennel Club
1-5 Clarges Street, London, W1J 8AB
Tel: 0870 606 6750
Fax: 0207 518 1058
Web: www.the-kennel-club.org.uk

To obtain up-to-date contact information for the following breed clubs, contact the Kennel Club:
• Beagle Association
• Beagle Club
• Beagle Club Of Northern Ireland
• Devon, Cornwall & South West Beagle Society
• Four Counties Beagle Club
• Northern & Midland Counties Beagle Club
• Scottish Beagle Club
• Welsh Beagle Club
• West Mercia Beagle Club

Beagle Advice and Welfare
Email: info@beagleadvice.org.uk
Web: www.beagleadvice.org.uk

USA
American Kennel Club (AKC)
5580 Centerview Drive,
Raleigh, NC 27606, USA.
Tel: 919 233 9767
Fax: 919 233 3627
Email: info@akc.org
Web: www.akc.org

United Kennel Club (UKC)
100 E Kilgore Rd, Kalamazoo,
MI 49002-5584, USA.
Tel: 269 343 9020
Fax: 269 343 7037
Web:www.ukcdogs.com/

National Beagle Club of America, Inc.
Web: http://clubs.akc.org/NBC/

For contact details of regional clubs and rescue organisations, please contact the National Beagle Club of America.

AUSTRALIA
Australian National Kennel Council (ANKC)
The Australian National Kennel Council is the administrative body for pure breed canine affairs in Australia. It does not, however, deal directly with dog exhibitors, breeders or judges. For information pertaining to breeders, clubs, shows, or bvreed rescued, please contact the relevant State or Territory Controlling Body.

Dogs Australian Capital Teritory
PO Box 815, Dickson ACT 2602
Tel: (02) 6241 4404
Fax: (02) 6241 1129
Email: administrator@dogsact.org.au
Web: www.dogsact.org.au

Dogs New South Wales
PO Box 632, St Marys, NSW 1790
Tel: (02) 9834 3022 or 1300 728 022
Fax: (02) 9834 3872
Email: info@dogsnsw.org.au
Web: www.dogsnsw.org.au

Dogs Northern Territory
PO Box 37521, Winnellie NT 0821
Tel: (08) 8984 3570
Fax: (08) 8984 3409
Email: admin@dogsnt.com.au
Web: www.dogsnt.com.au

Dogs Queensland
PO Box 495, Fortitude Valley Qld 4006
Tel: (07) 3252 2661
Fax: (07) 3252 3864
Email: info@dogsqueensland.org.au
Web: www.dogsqueensland.org.au

Dogs South Australia
PO Box 844
Prospect East SA 5082
Tel: (08) 8349 4797
Fax: (08) 8262 5751
Email: info@dogssa.com.au
Web: www.dogssa.com.au

Tasmanian Canine Association Inc
The Rothman Building
PO Box 116
Glenorchy Tas 7010
Tel: (03) 6272 9443
Fax: (03) 6273 0844
Email: tca@iprimus.com.au
Web: www.tasdogs.com

Dogs Victoria
Locked Bag K9
Cranbourne VIC 3977
Tel: (03)9788 2500
Fax: (03) 9788 2599
Email: office@dogsvictoria.org.au
Web: www.dogsvictoria.org.au

Dogs Western Australia
PO Box 1404
Canning Vale WA 6970
Tel: (08) 9455 1188
Fax: (08) 9455 1190
Email: k9@dogswest.com
Web: www.dogswest.com

INTERNATIONAL
Fédération Cynologique Internationalé (FCI)/World Canine Organisation
Place Albert 1er, 13, B-6530 Thuin,
Belgium.
Tel: +32 71 59.12.38
Fax: +32 71 59.22.29
Web: www.fci.be/

TRAINING AND BEHAVIOUR

UK
Association of Pet Dog Trainers
PO Box 17, Kempsford, GL7 4WZ
Telephone: 01285 810811
Email: APDToffice@aol.com
Web: http://www.apdt.co.uk

Association of Pet Behaviour Counsellors
PO BOX 46, Worcester, WR8 9YS
Telephone: 01386 751151
Fax: 01386 750743
Email: info@apbc.org.uk
Web: http://www.apbc.org.uk/

USA
Association of Pet Dog Trainers
101 North Main Street, Suite 610
Greenville, SC 29601, USA.
Tel: 1 800 738 3647
Email: information@apdt.com
Web: www.apdt.com/

American College of Veterinary Behaviorists
College of Veterinary Medicine, 4474 Tamu,
Texas A&M University
College Station, Texas 77843-4474
Web: http://dacvb.org/

American Veterinary Society of Animal Behavior
Web: www.avsabonline.org/

AUSTRALIA
APDT Australia Inc
PO Box 3122, Bankstown Square, NSW 2200,
Email: secretary@apdt.com.au
Web: www.apdt.com.au

Canine Behaviour
For details of regional behvaiourists, contact the relevant State or Territory Controlling Body.

ACTIVITIES

UK
Agility Club
http://www.agilityclub.co.uk/

British Flyball Association
PO Box 990, Doncaster, DN1 9FY
Telephone: 01628 829623
Email: secretary@flyball.org.uk
Web: http://www.flyball.org.uk/

USA
North American Dog Agility Council
P.O. Box 1206, Colbert,
OK 74733, USA.
Web: www.nadac.com/

North American Flyball Association, Inc.
1333 West Devon Avenue, #512
Chicago, IL 60660

Tel/Fax: 800 318 6312
Email: flyball@flyball.org
Web: www.flyball.org/

AUSTRALIA
Agility Dog Association of Australia
ADAA Secretary, PO Box 2212,
Gailes, QLD 4300, Australia.
Tel: 0423 138 914
Email: admin@adaa.com.au
Web: www.adaa.com.au/

**NADAC Australia (North American Dog
Agility Council - Australian Division)**
12 Wellman Street, Box Hill South, Victoria
3128, Australia.
Email: shirlene@nadacaustralia.com
Web: www.nadacaustralia.com/

Australian Flyball Association
PO Box 4179, Pitt Town, NSW 2756
Tel: 0407 337 939
Email: info@flyball.org.au
Web: www.flyball.org.au/

INTERNATIONAL

World Canine Freestyle Organisation
P.O. Box 350122, Brooklyn, NY 11235-2525,
USA
Tel: (718) 332-8336
Fax: (718) 646-2686
Email: wcfodogs@aol.com
Web: www.worldcaninefreestyle.org

HEALTH

UK
Alternative Veterinary Medicine Centre
Chinham House, Stanford in the Vale,
Oxfordshire, SN7 8NQ
Tel: 01367 710324
Fax: 01367 718243
Web: www.alternativevet.org/

British Small Animal Veterinary Association
Woodrow House, 1 Telford Way,
Waterwells Business Park, Quedgeley,
Gloucestershire, GL2 2AB
Tel: 01452 726700
Fax: 01452 726701
Email: customerservices@bsava.com
Web: http://www.bsava.com/

Royal College of Veterinary Surgeons
Belgravia House, 62-64 Horseferry Road,
London, SW1P 2AF
Tel: 0207 222 2001
Fax: 0207 222 2004
Email: admin@rcvs.org.uk
Web: www.rcvs.org.uk

Animal Health Trust
Lanwades Park, Kentford, Newmarket, Suffolk,
CB8 7UU.
Tel: 01638 751000

Fax: 01638 750410
Email: info@aht.org.uk
Web: www.aht.org.uk/

USA
**American Holistic Veterinary Medical
Association**
2218 Old Emmorton Road
Bel Air, MD 21015
Tel: 410 569 0795
Fax 410 569 2346
Email: office@ahvma.org
Web: www.ahvma.org/

American Veterinary Medical Association
1931 North Meacham Road, Suite 100,
Schaumburg, IL 60173-4360, USA.
Tel: 800 248 2862
Fax: 847 925 1329
Web: www.avma.org

American College of Veterinary Surgeons
19785 Crystal Rock Dr, Suite 305
Germantown, MD 20874, USA.
Tel: 301 916 0200
Fax: 301 916 2287
Email: acvs@acvs.org
Web: www.acvs.org/

AUSTRALIA
Australian Holistic Vets
Web: www.ahv.com.au/

**Australian Small Animal Veterinary
Association**
40/6 Herbert Street, St Leonards, NSW 2065,
Australia.
Tel: 02 9431 5090
Fax: 02 9437 9068
Email: asava@ava.com.au
Web: www.asava.com.au

Australian Veterinary Association
Unit 40, 6 Herbert Street, St Leonards, NSW
2065, Australia.
Tel: 02 9431 5000
Fax: 02 9437 9068
Web: www.ava.com.au

Australian College Veterinary Scientists
Building 3, Garden City Office Park,
2404 Logan Road, Eight Mile Plains,
Queensland 4113, Australia.
Tel: 07 3423 2016
Fax: 07 3423 2977
Email: admin@acvs.org.au
Web: http://acvsc.org.au

ASSISTANCE DOGS

UK
Canine Partners
Mill Lane, Heyshott, Midhurst, GU29 0ED
Tel: 08456 580480
Fax: 08456 580481
Web: www.caninepartners.co.uk

Dogs for the Disabled
The Frances Hay Centre, Blacklocks Hill,
Banbury, Oxon, OX17 2BS
Tel: 01295 252600
Web: www.dogsforthedisabled.org

Guide Dogs for the Blind Association
Burghfield Common, Reading, RG7 3YG
Tel: 01189 835555
Fax: 01189 835433
Web: www.guidedogs.org.uk/

Hearing Dogs for Deaf People
The Grange, Wycombe Road, Saunderton,
Princes Risborough, Bucks, HP27 9NS
Tel: 01844 348100
Fax: 01844 348101
Web: www.hearingdogs.org.uk

Pets as Therapy
14a High Street, Wendover, Aylesbury, Bucks.
HP22 6EA.
Tel: 01845 345445
Fax: 01845 550236
Web: http://www.petsastherapy.org/

Support Dogs
21 Jessops Riverside, Brightside Lane, Sheffield,
S9 2RX
Tel: 01142 617800
Fax: 01142 617555
Email: supportdogs@btconnect.com
Web: www.support-dogs.org.uk

USA
Therapy Dogs International
88 Bartley Road, Flanders, NJ 07836,.
Tel: 973 252 9800
Fax: 973 252 7171
Web: www.tdi-dog.o

Therapy Dogs Inc.
P.O. Box 20227, Cheyenne, WY 82003.
Tel: 307 432 0272.
Fax: 307-638-2079
Web: www.therapydogs.com

Delta Society - Pet Partners
875 124th Ave NE, Suite 101, Bellevue, WA
98005 USA.
Email: info@DeltaSociety.org
Web: www.deltasociety.org

Comfort Caring Canines
8135 Lare Street, Philadelphia, PA 19128.
Email: ccc@comfortcaringcanines.org
Web: www.comfortcaringcanines.org/

AUSTRALIA
AWARE Dogs Australia, Inc
PO Box 883, Kuranda, Queensland, 488..
Tel: 07 4093 8152
Web: www.awaredogs.org.au/

Delta Society — Therapy Dogs
Web: www.deltasociety.com.au